YOSEMITE MAASAI

A Biography of an Unexpected Life

I0521624

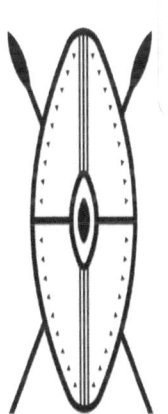

Rachel Mazur

Wild Bear Press
Washington, USA

This book is a biography. It is based on dozens of interviews with Olotumi Laizer as well as extensive background research. The completed book does not represent the views of all Maasai but, rather, those of Olotumi Laizer.

Library of Congress Cataloging-in-Publication data is available upon request.

ISBN 979-8-9850157-0-6 (paperback)
ISBN 979-8-9850157-1-3 (ebook)

First edition 2021
10 9 8 7 6 5 4 3 2 1

WILD BEAR
PRESS

With love for our mothers:
Naalamala and Polly

Preface

IN 2016, I TRAVELED TO TANZANIA with Olotumi Laizer, known as "Laizer," as part of a three-person contingent sent to set up a sister-park agreement between Yosemite National Park and Ngorongoro Conservation Area. I was selected as a Yosemite representative because I supervised Yosemite's wildlife program and had previous experience traveling in East Africa. Laizer was selected because he was born in Ngorongoro and would be instrumental in translating language, cultural norms, and expectations. Laizer also initiated the whole idea of joining the two parks. Together, we traveled with Linda Mazzu, who was the supervisor of Yosemite's Division of Resources Management and Science.

While in Tanzania, we had the opportunity to visit the traditional Maasai village of Naiyobi, where Laizer grew up. Bumping along the muddy roads to Naiyobi, we traveled from one already-remote location to an even more remote one. The four-hour trek took us through stunning, wildlife-rich scenery. Upon our arrival, a giggling horde of children from the village greeted us, as well as a few of Laizer's friends. They all pitched in to help us carry the fifty-pound bags of rice we'd brought for Laizer's mother. Together, we walked the mile and a half up a rutted dirt path to her mud-and-cattle-dung home.

When we arrived, Laizer's mother greeted us with a warm smile, which grew brighter when she laid eyes on her firstborn son. Then some villagers showed up shouldering the rice, and Laizer's mother turned to the dozen or so Maasai women who now circled her and quickly divided up the rice. What I'd thought would be a few months' supply ended up being no more than a small bowlful for each person.

Alarmed, I asked Laizer if his mother had other stored grains. He brought me out of the bright sun and into her cool, dark home to show me her one shelf that held just one bowl with roughly two cups of grain inside it. There was no other stored food. This was the first time I had come face to face with a culture that truly lived from moment to moment and with no mechanism to prepare for unexpected hardship. Evidence of hardship wasn't difficult to find, as many of the people I met were coping with hunger, illness, and other stressors.

While traveling together, Laizer and I became friends. When we returned, I often asked him to tell me more about his Maasai childhood. I found it intriguing that after growing up in a remote, traditional Maasai village in Tanzania, his life's path had led him to work in Yosemite National Park in the United States. It was fascinating to watch him move seamlessly between the two worlds while bravely shouldering great emotional burdens and family responsibilities. As an author of several books, including an oral history, I couldn't help but want to capture his story. Luckily, Laizer enjoyed talking about his adventures and was eager to teach his American friends about the land of his birth and his tribal culture. About a year after our return, Laizer and I started this project.

To prepare, I dove into the world of the Maasai by reading books, scouring scholarly publications, and watching documentaries. Then I got personal. I interviewed some of Laizer's friends and family, and, most importantly, I interviewed Laizer. Over several years, we sat and talked dozens of times. In some cases, I asked him to tell me the same story multiple times to make sure I got it right. Laizer also read through the manuscript to check for errors and make sure I was representing his perspective throughout. What follows is the product of that effort. This is not meant to represent the views of the Maasai people. It is only meant to represent the views of Laizer.

Please note: Italicized terms are those Laizer commonly says in the Maasai language of Maa. Words in Swahili, the official language of Tanzania, are noted parenthetically.

Tanzania

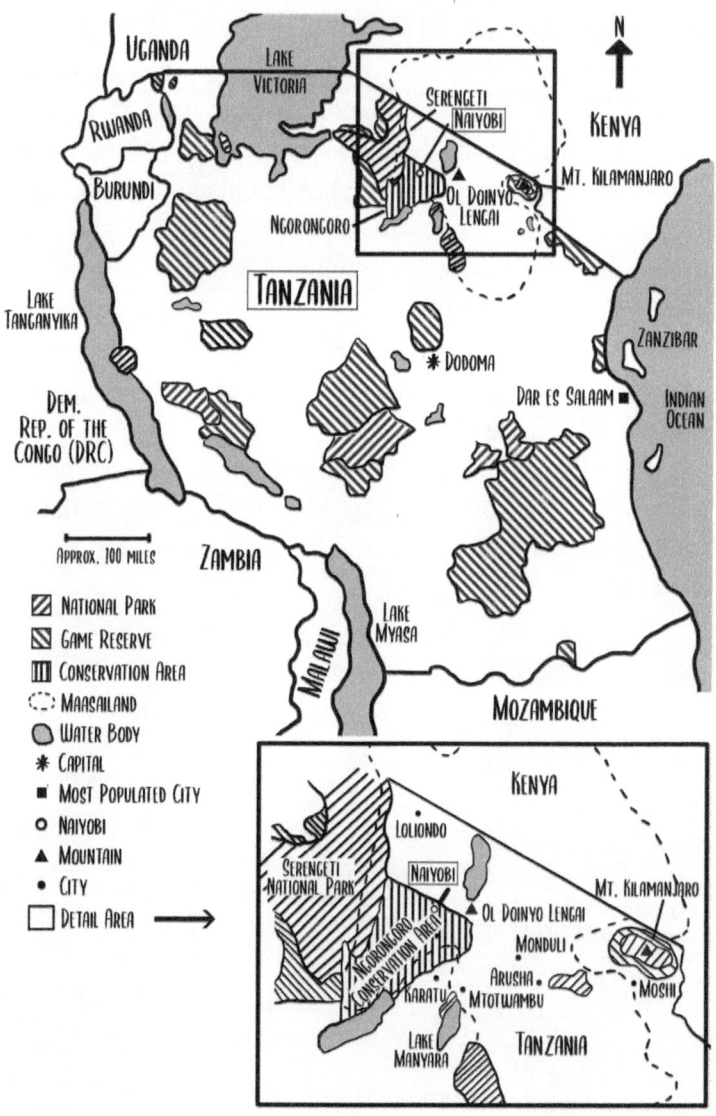

California

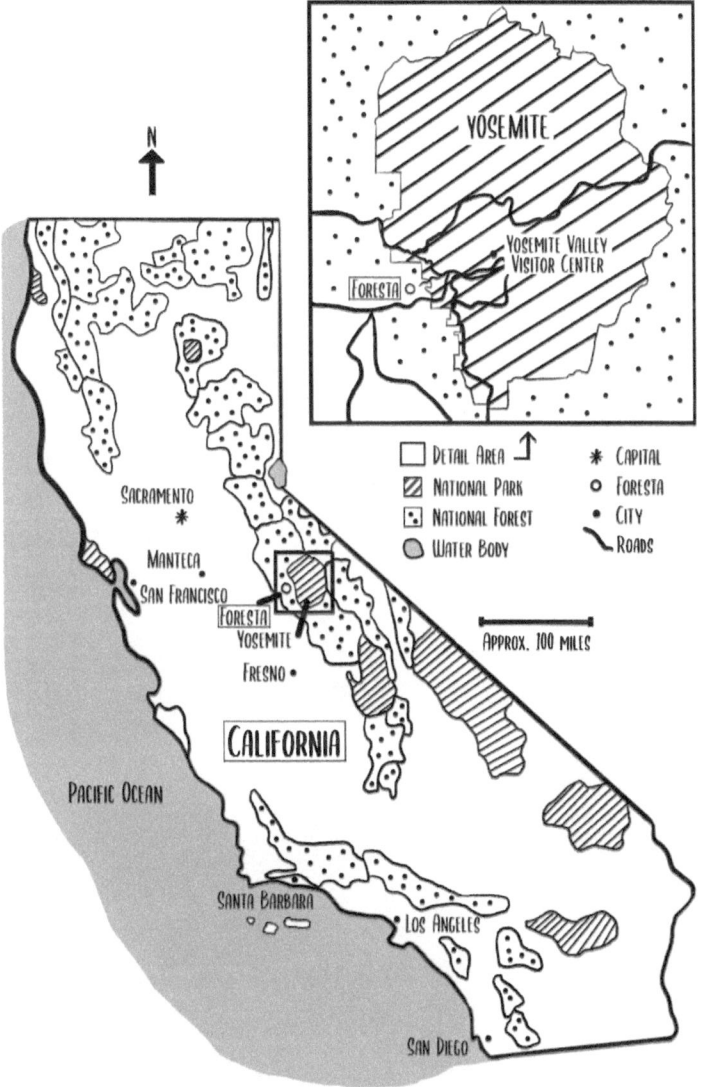

1

Dripping in sweat, Naalamala gritted her teeth as the pain of another contraction seized her body. As she labored, local women surrounded her, encouraging her with their prayers and song in the dark, smoky *enkaji*. Her mother-in-law, Mosari, a seasoned midwife, entered just as Naalamala stifled a scream when another contraction began. Mosari knelt down to massage Naalamala's abdomen and manipulated the baby into its proper head-down position. She then coached Naalamala to keep bearing down, even as pain and nausea racked her body. Finally, with one last push, Naalamala welcomed her first child into the world. A son. One who would grow to be humble and resilient like his mother while shouldering great responsibilities like his father.

On the day of his birth, however, the baby was so vulnerable and tiny that he fit into the palm of his mother's hand. His tiny size had been intentionally planned to increase both his and Naalamala's chances of surviving the birth. Not only do Maasai women living in this village in northern Tanzania have no access to medical care, but they also are married soon after puberty, before their hips are wide enough to safely give birth to full-sized babies. To keep her baby small, Naalamala was only allowed to drink broth and tiny portions of milk starting from the fifth month of pregnancy onward—a common practice in that region. Naalamala tried to comply, but she did occasionally sneak a bit of extra milk from the family's calabash. Luckily, she was never caught, or she would have been forced to vomit it up.

The hungry baby's first drink was milk from his mother; his hungry mother's first drink was blood from a bull. Had the baby been a girl, Naalamala's first drink would have been blood from a cow. Per tradition, her husband arrived after the birth to present the blood to Naalamala to help her regain her strength. Had the baby been born with a disability, he or she may have been left outside to die. Instead, he was the healthy firstborn son of Mekuru Laizer, who was also the village chief, so his birth was embraced and celebrated. Along with cattle, children are the wealth and pride of the Maasai people.

Mekuru provided five cows and five goats to be used for a celebration held the day after the baby's birth. Since livestock constitutes currency, Mekuru was displaying not only his wealth and status, but also honoring his good fortune in having a firstborn son. For a full day, the village gathered to celebrate, share meat, and sing. Neither Naalamala nor her newborn baby would attend. They stayed in the dark enkaji to rest and nurse.

With infant mortality a common occurrence among the Maasai, most parents wait until their babies survive three full moons to name them. Then, rather than the drawn-out process of choosing names that is common in western cultures, parents choose names spontaneously and often based on an observation someone blurts out. For that reason, the names may reference how a child looks, something that happened that day, or the weather. There is a child named "Head," because of an oddly shaped head; another named "Nose," for a big nose; "Angry," because of an impatient father; and "Rainy Day," for being born in such weather.

Mekuru and Naalamala didn't wait. They named their baby the day he was born because a friend had already blurted out a name for him. This happened right after Mekuru and Naalamala's wedding ceremony, when an inebriated friend declared, "I know you are going to get a kid tonight. Since it will be your firstborn, you will call it Olotumi if it is a boy and Natumi if it is a girl." Naalamala did become pregnant quickly, and, remembering the prophecy, the young parents named their son Olotumi, which simply means, "Firstborn." Olotumi now laments that he didn't get his first name from a relative or poem, but from a random remark made by one of his father's drunk friends.

Olotumi's second name, Mekuru, is his father's first name, as is dictated by tradition. It means, "It is not embarrassing," which makes one wonder what happened at his father's birth. Had Olotumi not been the firstborn son, his name would simply have been Olotumi Mekuru. In fact, all of his younger siblings have only first names followed by Mekuru. Since Olotumi was the firstborn son, he was honored with the addition of his father's second name as well, making him Olotumi Mekuru Laizer.

Naalamala also took her second and third names from Mekuru, making her Naalamala Mekuru Laizer. But she didn't begin the marriage with the name Naalamala; she came with the name Payaton Loriki. At marriage, however, Maasai women leave their entire past, including their first names, behind. They receive new first names in a manner similar to how babies are named.

For Naalamala, that happened right after her marriage ceremony, when Mekuru brought her to his mother's enkaji. Just before they arrived, a swarm of bees took up residence inside the enkaji, and there they remained there for eleven days. It was a gathering of bees, so Payaton was renamed Naalamala, which means "Gathering." Once Olotumi was born, Naalamala also was often called "Olotumi's mother," as birthing a son brought her honor, just as Mekuru was often called "Olotumi's father."

It is common across many cultures to honor a firstborn son by naming him after his father, but for the Maasai it holds extra importance. For once a Maasai dies, they are never spoken of again unless they have children to carry on their name. The firstborn son not only inherits his father's last name, but he also is called by it. Olotumi Mekuru Laizer is sometimes called Olotumi, but he is more commonly called Laizer, in deference to his father.

It is an honor to be called Laizer, and a big responsibility as well. It is a Maasai custom that when the father dies, the firstborn son must pay off his father's debts before taking the cattle his father has allocated to him, and then distribute any remaining cattle—or other wealth—among his siblings. He also inherits the responsibility of providing for his deceased father's wives and any children who aren't yet old enough to care for themselves. For Laizer, that number currently includes six wives and almost fifty children.

At the time of Laizer's naming, he was Mekuru's first and only child. He spent the first six months of his life nursing and bonding with his mother in her enkaji. Naalamala was able to spend much of this period resting with him—not because Mekuru took on her work, but because she'd had the foresight to gather six months' of wood before giving birth. Laizer's survival depended upon his mother's ability to provide him with milk, which she was more able to do with this critical period of well-deserved rest.

At the end of four months, Naalamala began to supplement Laizer's intake of her milk with unpasteurized cow's milk that she gathered each morning in her calabash. At the end of the six months, Naalamala returned to her work of gathering wood, carrying water, and milking the cows and goats, with Laizer tied to her back. He rode there until he took his first steps. Mekuru was not involved at all during this period. As a village chief, he spent his days presiding over village meetings, and at night he slept in the enkaji of his second wife, Noondomon, as she was his favorite. This was a welcome break for Naalamala, because Mekuru was demanding and would beat her at the slightest provocation. Naalamala had married Mekuru not out of love, but out of obligation to her own father, for he was the one who had arranged the marriage.

As a toddler, Laizer spent his days within his mother's *angan'g* (*boma* in Swahili*)*, the area that contained the enkajis of Naalamala, Mekuru's second and third wives, and Mekuru's mother. The angan'g was surrounded by an *enkang*, a thorny acacia fence meant to keep the family and young livestock safe from wild animals. Women built the enkajis; men built the enkangs.

The town held no other structures outside of these organically built homes that blended so well into the Serengeti Plains. Outside the *angan'g*, the presence of lions, hyenas, leopards, and buffaloes required constant vigilance. Within the confines of the *angan'g*, Laizer safely played with other toddlers and learned to care for the calves and lambs that were kept inside for safety.

When Laizer was four and a half, he was weaned from his mother's milk and began to rely fully upon cow's milk for nourishment. Luckily, those happened to be rainy years, allowing the cows to produce an abundance of milk. Also, there weren't yet a lot of siblings among whom to divide the milk. After Laizer's weaning, his grandma took him to her enkaji to sleep so Mekuru and Naalamala could once again share a bed.

Traditionally, Maasai spaced their babies at least five years apart, so the mothers could always carry their children as they moved from place to place. At his grandma's, Laizer and siblings from his two other mothers slept together on a wooden platform covered with a cow hide while his grandmother slept an arm's length away on her own cow-hide-covered platform. When he returned to his mother during the day, she would cover Laizer with kisses.

Laizer remembers this period as being a happy one; he had plenty of milk to drink and loved to play with the other children in the mud. His only possession, as was true of all the other children in Naiyobi, was his one red *orkarasha*, the brightly colored piece of cloth the Maasai drape over their bodies during all kinds of weather. Lazier felt safe and loved as he was always surrounded by family and under the protection of Ol Doinyo Lengai, or the "Mountain of God," an active volcano that sits at the edge of the village.

It was around this time that Laizer and the other boys began learning how to care for the goats. The boys also spent time pretending to be the strong warriors they would one day become. In doing so, they sometimes crossed the line of what was allowed—trying things like sneaking outside the angan'g and playing with sticks and knives. The boys were often away from their mothers' watchful eyes; the women were busy with chores and away for many hours of the day while collecting wood and water. In Maasai custom, however, all adults share the care of children, so whenever an adult was nearby, the children would be disciplined for any wrongdoing. Still, with sticks, knives, and little supervision, accidents happened.

Illness also happened and continues to happen. All Maasai have their lower incisors removed, not just for beauty and tribal custom, but also to ensure they can still be given milk in case of tetanus infection, which would lock their jaw muscles. Laizer remembers the searing pain from his aunt jamming and twisting an old metal spoon between his baby incisors until they popped out. Tuberculosis is another common disease, although it mostly affects women, as they are the ones who spend the most time in the smoky enkajis. Pneumonia and diarrhea are also prevalent; typhoid and cholera outbreaks are unpredictable; and trachoma, a bacterial eye infection that can be cured in first-world countries with antibiotics, comes all too often, usually leaving blindness in its wake.

The wildlife that lived outside the angan'gs also posed an ongoing risk of injury or death. While the warriors spent their time outside the angan'gs, tasked with keeping both the cattle and the community safe, it was critical to keep the children inside unless they were accompanied by adults. One method adults used to do this was scaring them with stories of what they could encounter on the outside. The main story Laizer remembers from childhood was about a giant half-human, half-metal beast called Nemulo, who would eat the liver of any human it found outside of an angan'g at night. Both children and adults believed this creature was real and were terrified of encountering it.

As a child, Laizer paid little attention to the women and even less to the girls. Ever since he could walk, he and the other boys were kept mostly separate from the girls. The boys didn't even know what the girls did during the day, and vice versa. They only spent time together at night, when they came together to sleep in a warm, safe pile of children in the enkajis. To Laizer, the girls seemed happy enough, having been trained to be subservient, never complain, and carry an aura of contentment. Because of the gender separation and the girls' training, there was no way Laizer could have known the intricacies of their days or of what they were learning—such as how to prepare for the beatings they would endure from their future husbands.

But there were things Laizer did notice. He noticed that the girls were always the first up and the last to bed. He noticed how far the girls walked during the dry season to get water (sometimes in the dark of night), how long they waited in line for their turns to let the water slowly drip into their plastic jugs, and how much the jugs weighed when they carried them back home, balanced upon their heads. He realized the danger the girls faced while washing the family's orkarashas in knee-deep water where hippos lurked. He also noticed that the girls always ate last. But while he saw these customs, he doesn't remember questioning them. He was simply following in the footsteps of Mekuru and the generations of Maasai that came before him.

Laizer also doesn't remember much about interactions with the one particular girl in town he was supposed to marry, for the arrangement was his father's choice and not his own. Before Laizer was born, Mekuru stated to a friend in the village, "When you have a daughter, I want her to marry my son." His friend agreed, and Mekuru presented his friend with a ring and nine cows to solidify the promise. There was no expectation of love or even friendship between Laizer and the friend's daughter; the arrangement simply held the expectation that the two children would join forces to carry on the Maasai traditions together. As such, while aware of one another, they each basically ignored the other, as they were busy with their respective childhoods.

2

CHILDHOOD PLAY MORPHS INTO SERIOUS RESPONSIBILITY at a young age for the Maasai. By the age of five or six, Laizer was no longer confined to his family's angan'g. Instead, he was sent out with other boys to keep the goats safe while the herd grazed in the grasslands around their village. The boys tracked their goats by name and color. Some boys were tasked with keeping goats in sight at all times while others served as lookouts for dangerous wildlife.

When wild animals appeared that might prey on the goats, the boys were expected to try scaring the animals away. If that didn't work, they were to run and get an elder to alert the warriors that help was needed. But the days were long, and the boys would grow restless. When they got distracted with play or adventure, they sometimes lost track of the goats and would have to find them or risk getting whacked with a stick when they returned home.

Occasionally, as the boys were watching the goats, they would see the Maasai warriors moving about in the distance. Sometimes it was just one, but more commonly it would be a small group of warriors. To the boys it was a magical sight.

Warriors were distinctive. Their lean, muscular bodies, hair braided with yarn, rapid strides, and long spears were stunning; and their bravery was legendary. On rare occasions, the boys even got to see the iconic sight of a line of warriors moving rapidly across the hillside to attend a ceremonial event. In those instances, the warriors would also be adorned with ostrich feathers and strings of colorful beads. Dozens of brave warriors in their full regalia moving confidently across the landscape—without even a sideways glance—was a sight Laizer and the other boys longed to be part of one day.

But until it was their time to serve as warriors, the boys contented themselves with the knowledge they learned from their fathers, which would keep them safe while watching the goats. This knowledge included an understanding of how each animal was most likely to attack and the basic skills needed to survive each type of attack. Because leopards and lions preferred to strike from above and didn't follow their prey up trees, the boys were taught how to scurry up branchless trees. Although the trees could serve as a refuge from these and other animals such as cheetahs and buffaloes, they would do nothing to keep the boys safe from elephants, which would just knock the trees over. Therefore, the boys were also taught how to use sticks and knives as weapons. Most importantly, fathers taught their sons how to identify the tracks and signs of dangerous animals and to always be aware of what animals were in the area.

The boys also learned about wildlife from observation. Every day, Laizer watched gazelles, flocks of lilac-breasted rollers, bushbucks, and the occasional golden jackal. His favorites were the zebras and the giraffes. Dozens of zebras were always around, and thousands more passed by in single-file lines, mixed with wildebeests during their twice-yearly migrations. Laizer and the other boys would sit and watch them pass by or try to scare them to make them move farther away. This was done to save the best forage for their cattle and to prevent any transmission of disease. Although giraffes traveled in smaller groups, they were equally mesmerizing to watch. Moving with a rapid long-legged gait, they appeared to flow across the plains. Laizer feared the buffaloes, as he knew they were extremely dangerous. As a boy, he rarely saw lions.

While the boys would collect ostrich feathers and porcupine quills for ceremonial decorations, they never injured the wildlife or tried to kill it to use as food. They were taught that Engai, their god, gave the Maasai, and *only* the Maasai, all of the cattle. Engai commanded the Maasai to eat only cattle, goats, and sheep. Although some Maasai villages do allow boys to eat wild animals for a short period right before their transition to manhood, Laizer's village did not.

All of the young males throughout the village were expected to spend their days tending the goats and sheep—with the exception of a handful of boys who were sent to a school by government decree. In 1984, when Laizer turned six, a small group of mud-and-dung buildings were erected in the center of Naiyobi to serve as a primary school, which was roughly equivalent to elementary school. Once it was built, a local man was hired as the teacher, and the school was opened to any child who was old enough. For the Maasai, who didn't record or acknowledge individual birthdays, children were determined to be old enough if they could reach one arm over their head and touch their opposite ear. Although primary school was free, all students were mandated to wear uniforms, which their families were expected to buy.

For families whose entire set of possessions could fit onto one chair, who knew nothing about a cash economy, and who hardly had enough cattle to feed themselves, the cost of one uniform was extreme. The burden was also pointless because a uniform for children in a rural Maasai school was simply a holdover from colonialism. The cost to the families of sending children to school, however, was much greater than simply the cost of the uniform—it was the cost of losing a valuable resource necessary to the functioning of their community. Without the children, there would be no one to care for the goats and sheep. There was also a cultural cost of having the government mandate how Maasai children were raised—a decision that traditionally belonged to the father. This decision would affect how children interacted with their fathers. As such, no one volunteered their own children to attend school.

As a result of local resistance to mandatory schooling for all children, the government resorted to requiring that one child from each family attend. A government officer assigned to Naiyobi went from angan'g to angan'g, collecting one child from each, until he had enough children to fill the school. Little did the government realize that the families were so reluctant to comply with its mandate that each one always sent its least favorite child. Since the school was small, it only affected about twenty families. Because Laizer's family wasn't one of them, he hardly gave it a thought—except that he had strong desire not to attend. School was of no concern to Laizer or his friends. Until it was.

It began one late afternoon when Laizer, at about ten years old, was out tending the goats at the edge of town. Daydreaming, Laizer gazed past the goats and up toward Ol Doinyo Lengai, the reassuring view that was reliably present in his life. Laizer startled and abruptly turned when unfamiliar voices entered his consciousness. A group of five white people and one black person—all wearing western clothes—approached him rapidly.

Laizer had heard of "blue-veined" or "white" people, but he had never before encountered one. He had also heard of western-style clothes, but he had never actually seen them either. When the group started waving and yelling at him in a language he didn't understand, he started to run. His speed in bare feet, however, was no match for the one black man's speed in boots, who caught up to Laizer and grabbed him by the arm. The man, who clearly wasn't Maasai—his earlobes weren't cut and his incisors were intact—spoke in Swahili. "We are not going to hurt you; we just need to find our campsite." Laizer, who only spoke Maa, believed the man was threatening to kill him and screamed while trying to get away.

The others soon caught up and started gesturing at Laizer with hand motions. They earnestly tried to make eye contact with Laizer. But Laizer, who had grown up in a culture where eye contact was only used in anger, looked away. The group continued to keep their eyes on Laizer and finally offered him candy. Never having seen or tasted candy before, Laizer's curiosity overtook his fear, and he calmed down enough to concentrate on what the group was trying to convey.

Eventually, Laizer understood their pantomime. The four German tourists and their Tanzanian guide from the Sukuma tribe were trying to find their campsite. Laizer knew where it was because he and the other boys had visited it in the past when no one was there. The campsite was rumored to be a place that was occasionally used by the more adventurous groups of foreigners, and now Laizer knew that was true.

Having no way to explain the directions to them and continuing to fear for his life, Laizer led the group to the campsite. He made sure to stay far ahead of them without losing them. It was about four miles and took over an hour. The group couldn't travel as quickly as Laizer was accustomed to moving, but he waited for them every time he got too far ahead. When they finally arrived, it was getting dark. Laizer quickly turned and headed for home. The group followed him.

Laizer was terrified because he had no way of knowing their intention. "Why do they want to kill me?" he muttered in Maa as he kept moving toward home. It was only later he would learn that they accompanied him to be sure he made it back home safely. Darkness had now completely settled across the plains, and a single child would be easy prey for the wild animals that often hunted at night. Only when the group saw Laizer safely enter his angan'g did they turn back toward camp. Laizer rushed through the gate designated for his mother and her children, noted that the goats had returned on their own, and scurried into his mother's enkaji. Without a word about what had happened, Laizer joined Naalamala on her cowhide-covered plank and slept with her as he had when he was a small child.

The next day, the Germans, the tour guide, and an additional man who was also wearing western clothing returned to the angan'g, trailed by curious villagers. Like Laizer, none of the villagers had seen white people before, or even people dressed in western clothing. Because the new man in the group could translate between Swahili and Maa, the Germans were now able to communicate with Laizer and his family. The Germans spoke to their tour guide, the guide spoke to the new man, and the new man spoke to the Maasai.

Through the translator, the group asked to meet the boy's father because they wanted to give a gift to the boy who had helped them find their campsite. One of the villagers quickly left and returned with Mekuru while Laizer emerged from the enkaji, doing his best to hide behind his mother. The tour guide addressed Mekuru through the translator, indicating the Germans would like to present his son with either a T-shirt, a piece of candy, or a piece of chalk, and asked which he would prefer. Mekuru didn't say a word but directed his gaze in Laizer's direction to prod him to respond.

Laizer considered his answer carefully. He wanted the T-shirt and candy, but he had seen other boys draw on their friends' faces with chalk while they slept. The urge to do the same and make people laugh was irresistible, so he went forward, took the chalk, and rushed back to his spot behind his mother. Through the guide who communicated with the translator, the Germans asked, "Why do you want the chalk?"

Laizer answered truthfully, and after the translator and then the guide relayed his answer back, the Germans erupted in applause. The Germans then gave Laizer the candy and the T-shirt to keep and handed out candy to all the other children who were present. The Germans, their guide, and the translator then quickly met with Mekuru, who was stoic throughout and remained silent even after the Germans left.

To Laizer, the whole experience had been terrifying and mysterious although he was happy with his gifts and the attention from the other village children. Without quite understanding what had happened, Laizer returned to his normal routine the next day. About a month later, Mekuru found Laizer out tending the goats. Mekuru's body was tense, and Laizer prepared to run away from a potential punishment. But Mekuru didn't punish Laizer, and his message was brief.

Staring into the distance, Mekuru informed Laizer that he would be starting at the local school the next day, where he'd learn Swahili. The Germans had paid for Laizer's uniform, and now the government officer assigned to Naiyobi was requiring him to attend school; noncompliance was punishable by a fine. Mekuru spoke slowly and placed a special emphasis on the word, "Swahili." He lifted his eyes to briefly glance at Laizer before turning and walking away without another word, leaving Laizer to wonder what it all meant.

3

To weigh the importance of this turn of events to both Laizer and his father, it helps to consider it within the context of the histories of the Maasai and Laizer's family. According to the version of the origin story Laizer learned as a child, Maasai life began when their god, Engai, opened the sky over the southern Nile and lowered Naiteru Kop, the first human, down to Earth. Naiteru Kop had three children. To the first, he gave an arrow, so he could become a successful hunter. To the second, he gave a hoe, so he could become a successful farmer. And to the third, he gave a rod with which to herd cattle. While versions of the creation story differ among Maasai villages, they all agree that the third child was the ancestor of the Maasai and that this is the reason the Maasai, and the Maasai alone, are responsible for all the world's cattle.

The Maa language contains over thirty words to describe cattle, and every aspect of traditional Maasai life revolves around cattle. Women are in charge of milking them, and men are in charge of herding them. They provide Maasai people with the milk, blood, fat, and meat that—through

Laizer's childhood—made up the bulk of their diet. Maasai use cattle urine as an antiseptic. They use cattle hides for clothing, shoes, and bed covers; cattle horns to carry liquids; cattle dung to build their homes; and cattle hooves to fashion rings and beads to be worn during special occasions. Cattle also serve as the Maasai's primary currency; payments in cattle are often required to solidify arranged marriages and settle fines.

Cattle, along with children, are often called "the wealth of the Maasai." With cattle comes a good life, respect, and the ability to barter. There are even blessed cattle. In Laizer's village, the best cows are white with many black spots. The best bulls have big, even horns. The health of the cattle depends on the forage, which depends on the rainfall, which depends on the moods of Engai. While the Maasai have only one god that dwells in both heaven and earth, he has a dual nature, one of which makes their lives rich and the other makes their lives almost unbearable.

Engai Narok, known as the black god, is Engai's benevolent side, and he brings the thunder and rain that are so critical to keeping the cattle healthy. *Engai Nanyokie*, the red god, is Engai's vengeful side, and he brings lightning and drought. The length and intensity of the wet season and the dry, or "starvation," season, are controlled by Engai's moods. The Maasai elders sit under acacia trees to hear Engai's messages and then communicate them to the tribe. To stay on Engai's benevolent side, women pray and sacrifice milk to him every time they milk their animals.

The Maasai depend on warriors both to protect their cattle and conduct raids to pilfer cattle from others. This leads to a question: How could a widely dispersed population clustered into small villages develop a strong, rapidly deployable army? The Maasai solution, which was adopted from those of other East African tribes, is to divide their society into "age sets." Rather than focusing on individuals, males are grouped into age sets, each of which takes a turn serving as an army of warriors. Warriors serve their community for many years and then train the next age set to take over. When an age set of warriors retires, it transitions to a set of junior elders and, eventually, elders.

While age is one requirement to become a warrior, it doesn't ensure the warrior will be strong, committed, and fearless. To test for these desired traits and screen out those who don't develop them, the Maasai adopted another tradition from neighboring tribes: ceremonial circumcision. Ceremonial circumcision is done with no painkillers or antiseptic and involves ten cuts to the penis, during which a boy cannot cry, moan, or even twitch. If he fails, he may be ostracized from the village, beaten, or even killed. But if he passes, he goes on to be trained as a warrior. A single knife is used for the procedure on all of the initiates after being sharpened just one time.

Like cattle, warriorhood is central to the Maasai because of their belief that the Maasai are the caretakers of all the world's cattle. Indeed, the Maasai's intricate relationship with cattle can be traced through their history. According to the oral tradition in Laizer's family, the Maasai culture originated in Southern Sudan, which in Maa means "Ostrich Place," sometime in the 15th century, roughly four hundred years ago. From there they made it to what is present-day Ethiopia, which in Maa means "Elephant Land," and then farther south to the Great Rift Valley near Lake Turkana in present-day Kenya.

While there isn't solid evidence of the migration route recorded by oral tradition, it is fairly well accepted that the Eastern Nilotes, which included the Maa speakers, migrated into the Turkana Basin from the north and then spread east toward Mount Kenya. It is likely the Maasai derived their language, Maa, from the eastern Nilotic people who were living in what is now the country of South Sudan during this migration. It is also possible the Maasai adopted their age-set and circumcision rituals from the Cushites of southern Ethiopia as they moved south, although this latter point is more questionable, as evidence is scant and other tribes also practice these rituals who may have passed them on.

When the Maasai arrived in the area that is now Kenya, they were relative newcomers. They joined many other groups, including the indigenous hunter-gatherers and the agriculturalists, the latter of whom had long before migrated in from West Africa. Notably, all three groups of Naiteru Kop's children—the holders of the arrow, hoe, and cattle—were latecomers in comparison to the australopithecines, whose footprints from 3.6 million years ago were found by anthropologist Mary Leakey at Laetoli in northern Tanzania, not far from where the story of Olotumi Laizer begins.

In this new land, the Maasai entered Nairobi, which had a cooler climate than the lands to the north. The Maasai adapted. Continuing to shepherd, the Maasai shifted to a semipastoral lifestyle, adding the cultivation of millet and sorghum to their routine. When needed, the men would also trade with other tribes, occasionally even exchanging wives and children for agricultural products. Over time, the Maasai grew stronger until, about two hundred years ago (between

1840 and 1880), they began to dominate the area that is now Kenya and northern Tanzania.

The success of the Maasai was due to multiple factors. First, the Maasai gained hardy breeds of disease-resistant cattle. Second, they developed the age sets that allowed them to quickly mobilize armies of warriors from a widely dispersed area. Third, they obtained the iron technology needed to create larger spears for their armies. These factors allowed the Maasai to expand in strength and number despite paleoclimatological data indicating a concurrent drying of the climate. The warriors then secured coveted pastureland by pushing other tribes off the land, including from the Serengeti Plain.

By the mid-nineteenth century, the Maasai were at the peak of their power. Maasailand was seven hundred miles north to south, two hundred miles east to west, and broken geographically into twelve tribal groups called "sections." The Maasai were so dominant—and the warriors so feared—they were largely untouched by the slave trade that came through at that time.

With so much control over pasturage, most Maasai sections abandoned the agricultural lifestyle and became fully pastoral; their lives completely focused on moving cattle across the plains with the rhythms of the seasons. Laizer's family's section, the Kisongo, was one of the sections that became completely pastoral. A few other sections, particularly those living at the edges of the plains, continued life as semipastoralists. The Mwaarusha, for example, lived at the eastern edge of the plains and increasingly focused on agriculture. As such, each section developed somewhat differently while continuing to have access to what it needed through trade. Some Kisongo, for example, would give "surplus people" to the Mwaarusha in exchange for agricultural food. The Mwaarusha would benefit by getting wives and agricultural workers from the Kisongo.

Meanwhile, the Europeans were gaining power and land in Africa through the middle of the nineteenth century. From 1840 to 1890, the British ruled the Zanzibar Archipelago, which had been the center of Arab trade in slaves, ivory, and cloves. At first, the Maasai held strong, but that ended abruptly in the 1880s and early 1890s, when contagious bovine pleuropneumonia caused widespread cattle death and, subsequently, a major famine across Maasailand. After the famine, the Maasai were beset by cholera, smallpox, and a cattle plague called "rinderpest," which came from across the Red Sea. This triad of disease devastated the Maasai. Within a ten-year period, between one-half and two-thirds of the people and between eighty and ninety percent of cattle were dead. Severely weakened, the Maasai were then attacked by neighboring tribes who desired their territory and cattle.

The Europeans, now able to overtake the Maasai, divided up East Africa. This included drawing a horizontal line from Lake Victoria to the Indian Ocean—the only curve around the northern edge of Mount Kilimanjaro. This effectively divided Maasailand in two. In 1918, the southern half of Maasailand became a British mandated territory, which they named "Tanganyika." After the Europeans took the once-open plains into their control, the Maasai could no longer move nomadically across them or live wherever they chose. In the mid-1900s, the British created a series of parks in Tanganyika. In their attempt to protect the land, the British moved the Maasai out of their homeland and further restricted where the Maasai could graze their cattle.

One of the parks was Serengeti, which also happened to be where Laizer's grandfather was living. Wealthy by Maasai standards, Laizer's grandfather, Ngolenya, had seventeen wives. When the British moved the Maasai out of the new Serengeti Park in 1951, Ngolenya set off for the area around the Ngorongoro Crater, located within the Serengeti Plain but southeast of Serengeti National Park.

Ngolenya, fourteen of his wives, and several other Kisongo Maasai settled in Empakai Crater, just northeast of Ngorongoro Crater. He settled his three oldest wives further to the southeast, in Monduli, where the climate was warmer. But then in 1959, the British established the eight-thousand-square-kilometer Ngorongoro Conservation Area (NCA). NCA included the Ngorongoro Crater, the Empakai Crater, and Olduvai Gorge. The Maasai were allowed to remain in the NCA, but in 1975, they had to move out of the craters where they had found green grass year round and no mosquitoes. That also meant moving farther away from water sources. Luckily, Ngolenya's family found suitable land just north of the Empakai Crater, where they could survive by living seminomadically with a daily view of the volcano they named "Ol Doinyo Lengai." It was here that Laizer's grandfather and other Kisongo Maasai first established the village of Naiyobi.

Meanwhile, Tanganyika and Zanzibar gained independence from the British in 1961 and 1963, respectively, and they joined in 1964 to form the United Republic of Tanzania. In this new country, where over 125 tribes lived and spoke almost as many languages, the new president, Nyerere, decided there would be one cultural identity. To achieve this, he established Swahili as the national language. In a story common to so many cultures, children were sent to schools far from their homes to study languages other than their native language, in this case Swahili, and lost connections to their own families, communities, languages, and cultures. Although some say the tribal mixing led to less intertribal hostilities, it came at a great cost.

While many tribes began to assimilate, the Maasai that lived far from urban centers maintained their pastoral lifestyle. For most Maasai, some amount of modern culture crept in. Glass beads replaced bone beads. Cloth orkarashas replaced cowhide orkarashas. But even when the Maasai of Kenya began to assimilate, several of the Tanzanian sections of the Maasai, including the Kisongo, did not. Most Kisongo Maasai resisted, remained on the plains, and maintained their pastoral lifestyle. This was true even after the government tried relocating them into developed villages.

And so when tourists came to visit the NCA to see the famous crater, the footsteps at Laetoli, and the wildlife migration, they also came to see the tribe who lived among the wild animals, as if frozen in time. Soon the government realized that the Maasai were an attraction with potentially positive economic benefits. Quickly, the government reversed course from assimilating the Maasai and instead attempted to prevent the Maasai from changing at all.

When the government of Tanzania created the NCA, it also created the Ngorongoro Conservation Area Authority (NCAA) to manage the NCA. One of the objectives of the NCAA was to "safeguard and promote the interests of Maasai citizens," whose population at that time numbered somewhere between ten thousand and twenty thousand. As such, the NCA became the only conservation area in Tanzania that protected wildlife while allowing for human habitation. This, in part, is what made the NCA eligible to be designated as a UNESCO World Heritage Site in 1979. However, starting in 1975, the NCAA required the Maasai to either live as pure pastoralists or move out, with no exceptions. That included a complete ban on cultivation of food crops; the Maasai were only allowed to graze their livestock.

To Ngolenya and his family, Naiyobi was home. So they stayed. They lived a purely pastoral life, surrounded by wildlife, steeped in their traditions, and watched over by Ol Doinyo Lengai. Without being able to cultivate food, life was hard, but they stayed. Although tourism increased in NCA over the years, hardly anyone ever came to Naiyobi. There was no road to the village, and the land was far too remote for most tourists. This was the life Laizer was born into just a few years after Ngolenya's death, which was sometime in the mid-1970s. This is also why, until Laizer met the German tourists who sent him to school at age ten, he had never met a non-Maasai person, never seen western clothing, never tasted anything other than mother's milk and products from cattle and goats, and never spoken anything except Maa.

4

LAIZER LOVED SCHOOL. ON THE FIRST day, the teacher, named Palanjo, let the boys spend the entire day playing games to get to know each other. Palanjo started the day by giving them a soccer ball and a bit of instruction. Then he stood back and let them experiment. Since it was the first time the boys had played ball games, Laizer remembers it as being a horde of students all chasing one soccer ball with no real idea of what they were doing but having a great time. Laizer also made new friends that day. One was Yohana, an outgoing boy known for his storytelling and quick laugh. Yohana quickly became Laizer's best friend.

Instruction started on the second day. Even though he lived relatively close to the school and only had to walk a mile and a half to get there, Laizer didn't arrive early enough to get one of the limited number of desks. Instead, he joined several others who sat cross-legged on the dirt floor. They waited expectantly while Palanjo passed out chalk and little boards on which to write. Palanjo himself had a large version of the same type of board at the front of the room. After calling the class to order, Palanjo started writing on the board and asking the boys to copy what he wrote.

Palanjo wrote each of the boys' names. Laizer looked at the carefully formed letters Palanjo wrote and tried to copy them onto his little board. The chalk was awkward to hold, and Laizer's letters looked nothing like what Palanjo had written. Yet Laizer was writing. And when it was finally his turn to learn to write his name, Laizer felt the thrill of adrenaline as he scratched out his own rendition of the word. The writing instruction continued until mid-day when Palanjo gave the boys a two-hour break to play soccer or practice throwing the sticks they had fashioned into arrows.

During this time, Laizer and some of the other students who were lucky enough to have brought a calabash filled with milk drank it as their lunch. Then it was back into the classroom to continue writing names and letters until five o'clock. Laizer was eager to learn his letters and remembers sneaking a book home to study. He was so captivated by the book that he memorized the whole thing in a week. Although Palanjo couldn't believe how fast he'd learned, Laizer never admitted to taking the book home. Instead, he just sneaked it back into the school.

Laizer quickly adjusted to the rhythm of the school day. He would rise early, drink the milk his mother had collected that morning, race the mile and a half to school to try and get a desk, spend the day there, and return home in time to receive milk for dinner. Being one of the oldest of the new kids in his class at the school never bothered him. He grew aware of his luck at playing games and sitting inside on rainy days instead of being outside watching over his family's goats. Laizer particularly remembers the days when the rain came pouring down while he was safe, warm, and dry with the other boys in the classroom.

Although there was a uniform requirement, students came to school in all manner of clothing, from the traditional ork-arasha to partial uniforms and full uniforms. It all depended on what the family could cobble together. The commonality was that whatever a student wore, he wore it every single day because that was all he owned. Having a sponsor, Laizer received a uniform of a dark blue button-down, short-sleeved shirt and light brown shorts during his second month of school, which he dutifully wore each day. By the end of the year, his uniform was nothing more than shredded rags. Laizer received a new uniform from his sponsor before the start of the next year.

There was also a certain drudgery to school—sitting still for endless hours listening to the teacher's lessons. Palanjo wasn't trained in teaching or even good at it; he'd gotten the job because he'd learned Swahili while enlisted in the Tanzanian war with Uganda. During Laizer's second year of school, he began receiving punishments, which diminished his enthusiasm for school. Once, he did poorly on a test, and Palanjo beat him. He also was once whipped by both his father and Palanjo for bringing nails and a mirror to school. Laizer's father had gotten the nails in Karatu to fix his beehives, but Laizer wanted to share them with the other students in order to repair their shoes. The mirror had belonged to his mother, but because the other students didn't believe there was an object they could look in to see their own reflections, Laizer brought it in to show them.

Beatings weren't new to Laizer. He had seen his father beat his mother on several occasions and had received plenty of them as well. He knew when they were coming by the look in his father's eyes. He always tried run away before his father could hit him. When he couldn't get away quickly enough, he would tolerate the beating without complaint but with anger silently brewing inside him.

During Laizer's third year of school, the Tanzanian government gave Naiyobi official recognition as a town and upgraded the school system. Along with building a new schoolhouse, the government brought in a trained teacher from outside the village. This teacher, who was not Maasai and did not speak Maa, would follow the mandate that all primary schools were to be conducted in Swahili. With so few children in school, Maa remained the primary language spoken in Naiyobi, but the students learned to speak and write in Swahili at school. The students were never taught in their native language, nor did they ever learn to write in Maa. Laizer used this training in Swahili to his advantage—he had acquired a secret language, one he could use when he wanted to communicate privately with one of his school friends, and one that would open doors for him later in life.

On Saturdays and Sundays, as well as the entire months of June and December, there was no school. During these times, Laizer and the other boys would help their families by taking care of the goats. During the rainy season, the boys were back out herding in the cold and rain, which made them anxious to get back into the shelter of school on Monday morning. More often, though, after spending all week in school, it was refreshing to be in the open air with nothing to do except be lost in one's thoughts or have adventures with each other, of which the boys had many. It was during these adventures that the boys made discoveries about the land, the wildlife, and even their own culture.

Laizer remembers one such discovery occurring when he was simply taking the family's goats for water. As usual, he'd traveled with the goats by staying within the center of the herd. Goats frequently were killed and eaten by wild animals, so the center of the herd was where Laizer's father instructed him to remain in order to stay safe. But it was difficult to see what was ahead while tucked safely within the group.

On that particular day, Laizer was frustrated with the goats because they wouldn't move forward. So he started hitting them with a stick to spur them on. Suddenly, a buffalo jumped up from in front of the herd and ran off to the side. Had Laizer not been tucked safely inside the herd, he could easily have been killed. Laizer learned to trust the goats when they wouldn't move and to trust his father that the middle of the pack was the safest place to be.

Laizer and his friends made another discovery while tending the goats. Exploring the plains for something to catch their interest, the boys came upon the dead body of a man they recognized. He was wearing a clean orkarasha, had his left arm tucked under his head, and was oriented toward the east. The Maasai oriented the bodies of their dead toward the rising sun as an offering to Engai, with the hope of bringing good luck to the family. Since the luck was dependent upon the body being consumed quickly by wild animals, they would also smear the body with fat and sprinkle grass on it to lure the animals in.

Laizer and his friends stared at the body and poked it with sticks. They sat to watch what would happen to it. When the sun slipped below the horizon, they had to leave the dead body so they could herd their goats—and themselves—home to the safety of their angan'gs. The kids returned the next day to find the body ripped apart, the stomach and intestines strewn across the plains. Nearby, a hyena greedily crunched through what appeared to be a leg bone. When they returned again the third day, the body was completely gone. The family of the man would be blessed with good luck while Laizer would forever be haunted by the image of the man who had been ripped apart and the sound of the hyena crunching his bones.

While thinking about that day still makes Laizer shudder, that experience taught him a great deal about life and death. He learned what it looked like to be dead. He learned what the Maasai traditionally did with their dead. He learned how quickly the local wildlife could consume human flesh, and how easily a hungry hyena could bite through a human bone. He learned how fragile life is.

Up until that time, Laizer had never thought much about death. In fact, he hadn't worried much about anything. Instead he'd lived day to day. During his happy childhood, he had a close relationship with his mother, his many friends, and school to keep him occupied. But on more and more frequent occasions, Mekuru would stare at his children and tell them to go outside. Although Naalamala wouldn't yell or scream, Laizer and his siblings knew exactly what was happening to her. In an attempt to stop Mekuru from beating Naalamala, the children would run and ask other adults to intervene.

Laizer was increasingly alarmed at how poorly his father treated his mother and how often he beat her, but he still saw Mekuru as a strong and protective father who kept his family fed. When he compared them to so many other families, Laizer was grateful that he always had enough milk. At least during the wetter years. But as Laizer learned, no matter how hard the women prayed, the years weren't always going to be wet, and hard times would come.

5

WHEN RAINS ARE GOOD AND FOOD is plentiful, Maasai eat. During droughts, when food is scarce, they don't. The Maasai of Naiyobi have no provision for catastrophe of any kind, including any kind of food storage. In the Ngorongoro Conservation Area, where Laizer grew up, the Maasai who lived within its boundaries were forced to be completely pastoral after the NCAA banned cultivation in 1975. The planting of crops was not allowed, even for backup supplies, forcing the Maasai to truly live a feast-or-famine existence.

In Naiyobi, until recently, milk was the main food staple. The Maasai drink it plain, curdled, and as a yogurt. During the rainy season, when cattle get plenty of grass, there is also plenty of milk. To keep the rain coming, Maasai women pray to Engai Narok every morning and evening when they milk the cows and goats. With every animal, they take the first bit of milk from each teat and toss it into the four directions, each time praying, "Engai Narok, please bring health to our children and our animals." During Laizer's early years, he loved milk and drank it for breakfast, lunch, and dinner.

Occasionally, Maasai need something more fortifying than milk. In those cases, they drink blood from their cattle. Blood gives them stamina and keeps them from getting hungry again for long periods of time. Women drink blood after giving birth, and all Maasai drink blood after circumcision or when they are very sick. It is most commonly drunk by warriors to give them strength and stamina for their stunningly long walks of thirty miles or more each day. Children have less need for blood meals but do drink it when they are hanging around the warriors.

To get the blood, the Maasai nick the jugular vein of one of their cattle with the tip of an arrow and then seal it off with dung. If the bleeding doesn't stop, they apply the hairy leaves of the *intulelei*. This plant is commonly called a "Sodom apple" in English, or in Latin, *Solanum incanum*. Since Maasai almost never drink water, they do not want to increase their thirst by drinking salty blood. Maasai don't take blood from cows that are mating or pregnant because they don't want to risk the cows' chances of getting pregnant or of carrying the young to term.

Maasai sometimes drink raw, liquid fat. Liquid fat is given to those who have been injured to stop the bleeding. When he was a child, both the fat and the blood made Laizer gag, but when it was given to him, he had no choice except to drink it. In those times, he tried to drink it quickly, as it tasted better and had less of a strong odor while it was fresh and warm. Regardless, it was still hard to choke down. He remembers drinking it like a young man drinking whiskey for the first time; he would slightly shake while forcing it down, hoping his facial expression wasn't revealing his strong distaste.

On the rarest occasions, Maasai eat meat. When they do, they don't drink milk with it because they believe it is wrong to eat products from live and dead animals on the same day. Everyone eats meat at ceremonies such as births and weddings, but the individual family's wealth determines how frequently meat will be consumed by that family at other times. Warriors eat more meat than any other Maasai, as they need to gain strength. Warriors even have meat-eating retreats, called *orpuls*, designed to build wellness and strength. Orpul can last for weeks.

Being the firstborn child in a relatively well-off family, Laizer remembers his father eating meat a few times a week and always saving a piece for Laizer. As more siblings came along, the portions got smaller, but everyone would get at least a bit because Maasai always share. Maasai not only share with family and friends, but also with strangers. They even designate certain cuts of meat for certain people. The only parts of livestock Maasai don't eat are the brain, lymph nodes, contents of the stomach and intestines, and eyes. Like many cultures around the world, the Maasai believe the eyes are the window to the soul.

Until recently, outside of cattle products and tea, the pastoral Maasai living in Naiyobi ate little else. The timing of when the Maasai drink milk versus blood, or when they eat meat, is dictated by tradition. The amount each individual eats is dictated by individual resources, the number of family members to feed, and, most importantly, the amount of rain. Because the rains generally come in October and last until the following spring, the hardest time for the Maasai starts in August and runs through September when the cows give less milk. October and November are almost unbearable because food can become so scarce that there simply isn't anything for the villagers to eat. There isn't even much to consume in the way of native plants. One exception is a reddish plant the Maasai call *mnafu*, which the women collect and cook to eat.

This is why the dry season is sometimes referred to as the starvation season; people are literally starving. Families with plenty of cattle can even suffer during these times, but they are at least able to add a little blood to their children's milk to reduce their hunger. That was how it was with Laizer's family. Families that don't have many cattle often resort to asking others to share or end up going hungry. Laizer remembers the stream of mothers coming to visit his own mother's angan'g with empty calabashes, hoping for milk for their children who were so hungry they couldn't sleep.

The horror of seeing others starving to death will never leave Laizer. The children cried from hunger until their legs became skeletal. When they got so malnourished that their empty bellies swelled, they would just lie quietly from exhaustion. Some of them died. Even as a child, Laizer shared his own meager ration of lunch milk with others to ease their pain. He also sometimes brought children to his grandmother's angan'g so they could drink milk because his family always had enough…until one day when they didn't.

It happened between Laizer's second and third year of primary school when little rain came. During that year, Laizer saw more children crying from hunger. The children were so hungry they would sit glassy-eyed and couldn't concentrate in school. Some didn't even have the energy to walk to school and back. During this particular year, there was simply nothing to eat, and people beyond just the young, weak, and very old were dying. Some days it seemed the whole town was just sitting from hunger and exhaustion, with the only human voices being the cries from starving babies. No one was immune, not even Laizer's relatively well-off family who was also overcome with hunger.

Luckily for Laizer, Mekuru had enough animals that he began to barter them for food. Every two weeks during that dry and dusty season, Mekuru walked a day and a half to a place along the Mosquito River near Manyara National Park and sold a cow for two hundred pounds of flour. He then walked a day and a half back with three donkeys carrying the flour and divided it among his wives. Naalamala mixed her portion of the flour with the water she'd walked miles to collect to concoct a tasteless, watery drink they called porridge. This wasn't the flour and water mix commonly known as *ugali* that is often consumed in the cities. This was a more watery version. Laizer remembers it tasting terrible, but he was also desperate to fill his belly. This was the first time in Laizer's life that he had consumed anything other than a cattle or goat product. It was also the first time Laizer remembers wondering why the Maasai had so many children when it was so hard to feed them all.

A few years later, when Laizer was about thirteen, the NCAA built the first rough dirt road into Naiyobi. This was followed by a small church and then a house for a pastor next to the church. These types of buildings and the jeeps that brought in the materials to build them were all new to the villagers. The first pastor, an American named Ned, was white, tall, and—as Laizer remembers it—hairy. But he had lived in Tanzania for many years, spoke fluent Swahili and Maa, and was kind to the students. At first, Laizer feared Ned, but he warmed up to him quickly because Ned was so friendly. Ned interacted with the students by asking them to help him carry water to his home or build a fire. In return, Ned gave them rice, beans, meat, ugali, and tea. Ned even had sugar for the tea. Laizer quickly learned to be fast and helpful so he would get invited over to Ned's a few days a month. In addition to sharing food, Ned tutored Laizer with his schoolwork.

As they spent time together, Ned spoke to Laizer about how he didn't agree with the way Maasai men treated their wives, how they married multiple wives, or how they had more children than they could feed. Ned asked Laizer how he planned to treat his wives. Laizer sat quietly, not knowing how to answer. What Ned was telling him was different from what he knew and different from what happened in his own family. During this time, Laizer wished to be a pastor like Ned, not because of Ned's religious leanings, but because it meant a house full of food and access to a car, two things Laizer knew he wanted. Ned also owned a few intriguing possessions, notably a radio and tape recorder, both of which Laizer would examine when Ned wasn't around.

Later that year, the NCAA grudgingly relaxed the restriction against cultivation in the NCA. Laizer's family, like so many others, quickly established gardens with corn, beans, and potatoes. Mekuru constructed a fence from wooden poles to keep out the wild pigs and porcupines—and the occasional buffalo. Just as the NCAA feared, the gardens lured in wildlife, and that led to some human-wildlife conflict. Although the impacts were mitigated with fences and Maasai attentiveness, some animals were killed.

Also, just as the NCAA feared, the allowance of cultivation increased the number of Maasai living in the NCA because some people who had moved away to cultivate outside the NCA now returned. But, thankfully, the main intention of allowing for cultivation—to reduce hunger—was successful. While hunger was still an issue, more of the Maasai had something to eat—including Laizer—who was now able to spend his teenage years with food in his belly.

6

JUST LIKE YOUNG TEENAGERS EVERYWHERE, MAASAI teens face peer pressure. Except in Naiyobi Laizer didn't face peer pressure from other teens to rebel against the customs of his parents. He faced peer pressure from other teens—and his parents—to participate in their tribal customs. Prior to attending school, Laizer would have done so without question, but after learning a bit about other ways of doing things from both Palanjo the teacher and Ned the missionary, Laizer started to consider not participating in all of the Maasai customs.

At the beginning of their teenage years, Maasai undergo the visible transformations that are part of being Maasai—getting their ears cut and their adult lower incisors removed. Ears are cut purely for cultural identity and beauty. The adult lower incisors are removed, just as the baby ones were, primarily for medical reasons but also for cultural identity and beauty. As is customary with all things Maasai, these traditions are done in age order, from oldest to youngest. As such, Laizer was slated to be the first in his family to get his ears cut.

However, Laizer didn't want his ears cut. Neither Palanjo nor Ned had had it done, and both told the students they saw no reason to do it. Based on their influence, some of the other schoolboys had already declined to have their ears cut. Laizer refused to have his ears cut until his younger sister had hers done and started taunting him about it. That put him over the edge. Since he couldn't be one-upped by his younger sister, he asked one of his uncles to cut his ears.

His uncle, Melani, who was more than willing to perform the ritual, came into Naalamala's enkaji with a bush knife. He pulled out Laizer's right earlobe, forcefully pushed the knife in, and twisted it until it cut through the flesh and cartilage. Sawing the knife up and down, Melani cut away a circular patch of skin, wider than his thumb, and let it drop to the floor. Blood poured from the wound and down onto Laizer's shoulders until Melani plugged it with a piece of wood.

The pain felt hot and seared across his head, but Laizer didn't flinch as Melani reached for the other earlobe and slowly did the same to it. To hide his pain Laizer stared straight ahead while his uncle explained how the lobes would later be stretched. Laizer had to be braver than his sister to avoid further taunts and didn't want to embarrass himself or his father by showing fear. That night, he writhed in pain. Unable to sleep on either side, Laizer laid on his back as the pain throbbed and robbed him of rest. But it was done, and, barring infection, it would slowly heal.

A few years later, it was time for Laizer to have his adult lower incisors removed. At first, Laizer refused the procedure even though his peers were taunting him. But Naalamala knew that the taunting by the other children would only increase, and she wanted to spare Laizer that humiliation. She told Laizer she would be sure one day it was done but didn't specify when. One day, one of Laizer's grandfathers arrived, told Laizer he was going to remove his teeth, and instructed Laizer to open his mouth.

Laizer tensed as he opened his mouth just far enough to allow his grandfather's bush knife inside. His grandfather then used the knife to press down on the gum beneath one of his front teeth. Laizer stared forward as his grandfather started cutting. Laizer stared forward even when his grandfather realized he'd wedged the knife under the wrong tooth, moved the knife to the correct position, and started cutting again. Laizer's muscles tensed, but he didn't flinch as his grandfather pried until the tooth popped out and then did it again with the second tooth. The pain was heavy and throbbed for a week, but Laizer never complained about the pain—or the mistake—to anyone, determined not to show any weakness. Once his gums healed, Laizer liked his new look and knew his parents were proud.

These rituals not only gave Laizer the look of the Maasai, but they also gave him much-needed practice in tolerating pain. For the day would come when Laizer would need to be able to endure his circumcision without showing any emotion. Some children and teens practiced tolerating pain by using burning sticks to sear designs into their skin, but Laizer never participated in that.

The teenage years are also a period when Maasai fathers typically give their sons tougher beatings than when they were children. This was certainly true in Laizer's case. Mekuru had taken to drinking a strong local alcohol made from sugar, and it made him angry and combative. The violence escalated further after Mekuru sold some of his cattle to start a business selling alcohol. With access to more alcohol, Mekuru started drinking on a daily basis. He would be gone all day and return home at night drunk, angry, and violent. His violence was aimed at everyone, family and friends. While the children would run away to avoid his wrath, Mekuru most often set his sights on Naalamala, who endured many of his beatings.

Maasai men are allowed to beat their wives and children, and women are taught by their mothers what to do "when," not "if," they are beaten by their husbands. When the beatings happen, women have little recourse. They can't fight back. If they leave their husbands to return to their parents, they are not allowed to remarry. Further, if they leave their husbands, they must also leave their children behind with their husbands, even if the children were fathered by other men.

Children have no recourse to defend themselves against beatings. This is even true of teenage boys who are physically strong enough but haven't yet been through ritual circumcision. Uncircumcised boys are also not allowed to defend their mothers or siblings. Not only is the father in charge, but Maasai are taught that beatings are an accepted part of life and not to be resisted.

Mekuru was strong, and he didn't hold back when he lashed out. Laizer became more aware of, and alarmed by, the severity of the beatings his father was giving his mother. He noticed other things, too. He noticed how early Naalamala was up and how late she went to bed. He noticed how she was always the last adult to eat and how she received the smallest portions. And even though he was generally kept separate from his sisters, he began to notice that their burdens increased as they approached puberty.

The focus for Maasai girls is to learn the jobs expected of women. This prepares them to work in the homes of the older men they marry after the girls reach puberty and are circumcised. The girls spend their days milking animals, walking to get water and wood, building homes, and taking care of children. When there is milk to warm or meat to cook, they are the ones stoking the fires in the enkajis and cooking the meals. The work is difficult, but the girls are taught to hide their emotions, be complacent, and never complain. Only with other women do females share their burdens and lift each other up through song. But Laizer could see that his mother was often beaten, and his sisters worked hard throughout the day.

Laizer wasn't alone in his observations of the violence and injustice. Ned, the pastor, began to speak more openly about his observations of how the Maasai women were treated. It was often the topic of the sermons that he preached to the schoolboys for two hours every Thursday. Ned spoke of the brutality with which some Maasai men beat their wives and the general oppression of Maasai women. He also taught the boys to question the system by teaching them how to cook, which, in Naiyobi, is even today strictly a women's role. Ned presented Christianity to the boys as a path to being better people. While the religious teachings didn't resonate with Laizer, the criticism of the treatment of women did.

One night during this period, Mekuru came home drunk—so drunk that he threatened Naalamala with a bush knife. Laizer knew that as an uncircumcised male, he couldn't stand up to his father. But he also knew in his heart that he had to protect his mother. He stepped between them and stood facing Mekuru—an unarmed boy facing an enraged man with a weapon. It was the first time Laizer had ever done such a thing: taking a stand against his father. Mekuru was furious and turned the bush knife on Laizer, his eyes blazing with rage and his muscles tense. Laizer held his ground. Although his heart was thumping in his chest, he was ready for his punishment. But it didn't happen. No blows came. Mekuru stared at Laizer without blinking. Then, without saying a word, he lowered his arm, turned away, and abruptly left.

Having crossed a line from which he could never again return, Laizer soon learned that his relationship with his father had changed. Instead of Mekuru treating Laizer as a favored son, he treated him with anger and a palpable disgust, which wore on the whole family. Afraid of a beating, Laizer avoided his father as much as he could. Laizer's relationship with his mother changed as well. After being defended by the son she was so proud of, Naalamala showed her gratitude for this new twist in subtle ways. One notable time was when Naalamala gave Laizer his very first pair of shoes.

It happened right after Laizer took his exams at the completion of primary school. Since the exams were not available in Naiyobi, the boys had to walk to Nainokanoka, about twenty-five miles each way. Accompanied by warriors for safety from wild animals, the boys walked there, took the exam for two days, and then walked the twenty-five miles back. Because Nainokanoka is at about 8,600 feet in elevation (compared to Naiyobi, which is at about 7,500 feet), there was frost covering the ground as they neared the town. In Maa, Nainokanoka means, "It is foggy," although Laizer has translated it to mean, "I am shivering." And shivering they were. In Nainokanoka, the boys slept in a dormitory with blankets, but each way on the roundtrip journey, the group only had their uniforms of shorts and short-sleeved shirts to cover them. Only ten of the fifteen boys wore shoes. Laizer was one of the other five.

Laizer remembers his toes being so cold he couldn't feel them and yelling out in pain as he walked. Many of the boys were struggling and begged to stop and rest to ease the pain, but the warriors urged them to keep walking so their feet wouldn't freeze. When Laizer returned home, he asked Naalamala for shoes: "Mom, if you love me, can you buy me shoes?" To this day, Laizer has no idea how she did it, but Naalamala gave Laizer his own pair of "Maasai shoes," which are made from tires and held together with nails. Laizer gratefully wore those shoes to insulate his feet from the cold and the sharpness of the ground until they were worn to bits.

7

ALTHOUGH LAIZER PASSED HIS EXAMS FOR primary school, he didn't do well enough to earn a scholarship to secondary school. Luckily, his sponsor decided to continue paying Laizer's way. No one from Naiyobi had ever gone to secondary school before, and now both Laizer and his best friend Yohana, who did receive a scholarship, were going. Secondary school was a big deal. Unlike primary schools, there were no secondary schools located within the village of Naiyobi, but rather in towns far away, where the students had to live during the semester. Yohana's school was in Karatu, thirty-five miles away, and Laizer's school, the Kilimanjaro Boys Secondary School, was in a town called Moshi, one hundred fifteen miles away—a two-day trip by foot and bus. There, he would study with students from a variety of tribes from all over northeastern Tanzania. There were a few other Maasai students, but none from traditional Maasai villages.

Like primary school, secondary school went from July to November and from January to May. Laizer would return home only in June and December. In addition to a uniform, Laizer needed tuition, food, and a mattress, all of which were paid for by his sponsor. Although the sponsor paid the school, the school didn't provide these necessities to Laizer. Instead, they simply gave Laizer the money he would need for his first six months of the school year. This totaled thirty-thousand shillings, which at the time was roughly equivalent to thirty-five U.S. dollars.

This was the first time Laizer had seen money, and it was handed to him in new five-hundred-shilling notes. Laizer remembers thinking, *Holy smokes, how did I get this money?* He received the money with no instruction and had no idea what to do with it. Luckily, one of the other Maasai students at the school, whose name was Noel, had grown up near Arusha and knew how to navigate city life. Noel mentored Laizer by helping him organize the money and taking him shopping for books, pens, a uniform, and city shoes. Noel also introduced Laizer to underwear, an item of clothing Laizer had never heard of before.

More exciting than having money for supplies, however, was the mattress. It was Laizer's first mattress, and he had the whole thing to himself. In no time, sleeping became one of Laizer's favorite parts of being away at school. Another of his favorites was mealtime. The school usually provided ugali with rice and beans. Many other students complained that the food wasn't good quality, was too salty, or wasn't cooked well. Indeed, it did tend to be full of maggots, but after enduring so many starvation seasons, Laizer was grateful for this sustenance.

Sharing was natural to Laizer due to his Maasai upbringing, and it sped up the process of being accepted and making friends. And Laizer needed friends. At the beginning of school, many of the students from tribes in the cities laughed at him. Laizer was older, had shown up in tire shoes, was one of only a few Maasai, and was the only Maasai to have both his ears cut and lower incisors removed. However, Laizer also was unique in having a generous sponsor, which meant he could buy soap and an extra set of clothes. Regularly loaning these items out was an easy way to meet people and make friends.

Not that Laizer didn't have problems. School tradition was that the new students were supposed to wash people's clothing and bring them what they needed. As an older student, Laizer refused these demands and sometimes fought to defend his decision. That didn't go over well with the other students. Once, another boy dumped an entire bucket of water on Laizer while he was sleeping. Another time, someone locked Laizer to his metal bed by winding a lock through his ear hole. Laizer woke in the night, and when he tried to roll over, he couldn't move. A schoolteacher had to saw the lock apart to release him. Thankfully, these instances were rare.

The students kept busy taking classes all day and studying at night. Many were also assigned jobs to keep the school running. Laizer was responsible for seeing to it that the rain-water trapped during the wet season would last throughout the dry season. His duties included distributing the water as well as policing its use. As a reward, Laizer was allowed to take as many bucket showers as he wanted. When there was free time, the students played soccer. Laizer enjoyed soccer so much that he tried out for the Tanzanian national team and was selected. Practice for the national team was held forty-five miles away in Arusha, and Laizer's school provided transportation biweekly so team members could participate.

Arusha was the first big city Laizer had ever visited, and it was an eye-opening experience. First, Laizer learned about city transportation. Most people walked or took a *daladala*—a public minibus. However, the daladalas were crowded, dangerous, and difficult for the old and infirm. They were also loud and belched black smoke into the busy streets. It was a far cry from the fresh air and wide-open plains of Naiyobi.

Laizer also learned about the typical jobs available to the Maasai who ended up in Arusha. Unfortunately, the good city jobs were only available to those who had connections, resources, or education. Untrained, uneducated, and in many cases unable to speak Swahili, Maasai men who ended up in Arusha worked as guards, which were boring, low-paying jobs with no opportunity for growth. Maasai women who came to the city desperate for work often ended up selling their bodies for money just to get food to eat. Some of these women contracted HIV and then brought it home to their families, as did so many of the men who traveled to cities for work.

HIV is a widespread issue in East Africa and quickly spreads through Maasai communities due to their polygamous structure. The combination of lack of work, a prevalence of disease, and an unfamiliar culture left many Maasai in Arusha suffering from hunger and boredom. In many areas, the poverty is still so extreme that the children don't even have old cans to kick around.

These observations solidified Laizer's commitment to his education and his tribe, as he resented the devastation he saw happening to tribal members in the city. However, his exposure to life beyond his village also led to his further questioning his tribe's customs, particularly the traditional Maasai treatment of women, including that of circumcision and early marriage.

Of particular influence was his new friend Julius, who was in some of his classes and on his soccer team. Julius was Maasai but less traditional and had grown up in Nainokanoka, a larger village than Naiyobi that had a central downtown with a food market. At the end of each semester, Julius would join Laizer on his trip home as far as Nainokanoka, and they would discuss the similarities and differences in their upbringing. During those talks, Laizer learned about Maasai families that were intentionally smaller than his own, maintained some traditions while dropping others, and allowed their offspring to arrange their own marriages. These discussions would start questions churning in Laizer's mind as he continued on to Naiyobi.

Always grateful to be back in the beauty of the Rift Valley, Laizer would find his mind juggling conflicting feelings of gratitude for home and feelings of unease with certain traditions observed there. Laizer kept mostly kept quiet about it, but when his father was physically abusive to his mother, Laizer's anger was increasingly palpable.

One day, when Mekuru told Laizer it was time for Laizer's future wife to be circumcised, Laizer could no longer hold his tongue. For the second time in his life, Laizer stood up to his father, saying he would not go through with an arranged marriage. Mekuru looked into the distance and quietly but firmly said that, in Naiyobi, no one had ever rejected an arranged marriage, and the chief's firstborn son would not be the first. Laizer remained firm in his conviction. He told his father that he didn't want to be unhappy like Mekuru and would not marry the girl his father had chosen.

Stunned, Mekuru turned and looked directly into Laizer's eyes. "Then who would you marry?" he demanded.

Laizer didn't flinch and he didn't run. "I will marry for love," he responded.

"Love?" his father spat.

"Yes. Love," Laizer responded resolutely. "You know love. You feel love for your children, and I will feel that for my wife."

Mekuru's eyes pierced Laizer's as he declared, "No. You will marry the girl I chose, and you will be the first of your brothers to marry, as all Maasai do now and have always done."

"I cannot," Laizer responded.

"I will punish you for saying that," Mekuru boomed before turning and walking brusquely away.

Laizer was terrified. In Naiyobi, such a threat meant a traditional beating was in store. A traditional beating was nothing like the beatings Mekuru dealt out to his wives and children. In a traditional beating, the one being punished was stripped naked with one's hands and legs tied together while being brutally beaten. It could lead to maiming, organ damage, brain damage, or even death. And to add shame to an already terrifying proposition, as with all Maasai deaths, if you die and don't have children, your name is never uttered again. Such beatings are saved for only the most severe crimes.

Fortunately, Mekuru's brother, Ole-Ngolenya, was visiting and intervened on Laizer's behalf, asking Mekuru not to do it. Ole-Ngolenya agreed with Mekuru that Laizer needed to have the arranged marriage but did not want Laizer subjected to the beating.

Mekuru agreed not to formally beat Laizer but shook with rage.

"You," Mekuru fumed, glaring at Laizer, "are now cursed with death." Mekuru removed a bead from his necklace and threw it aside. "This bead is you. You are no longer my child. And when you die, no one will cry for you, and no one will ever speak of you again."

Laizer stood still, but his heart was thumping in his chest. As he watched Mekuru turn and walk away, he felt a wave of nausea run through his body. The emotional pain of being disowned was far worse than any physical pain Laizer had yet endured. He was devastated. But just as Maasai women are expected to look content and never complain, men are expected to look stoic and never show pain or fear, so Laizer didn't utter a word as his world collapsed. He was now a refugee from his own family. He had to leave, but where could he go?

When Ole-Ngolenya left at the end of that terrible day, Laizer silently followed him from a distance, moving stealthily like the predators he often observed on the savannah. Ole-Ngolenya didn't realize Laizer was trailing behind until it was too dark and too late to turn back. He took pity on Laizer, allowing Laizer to travel home with him to Monduli and remain there until school started again at the end of the month.

8

DESPITE THE BROKEN RELATIONSHIP BETWEEN LAIZER and his father, Laizer's uncle, Ole-Ngolenya, convinced Mekuru not to punish Laizer if his son returned to Naiyobi. After that, Laizer started spending time back in Naiyobi during the two school breaks each year, seeing friends and family, much to the relief of his mother. While Laizer had to greet his father when he came home, he would otherwise avoid Mekuru by staying in his best friend Yohana's angan'g. Since both of Yohana's parents had died, Laizer was able to stay there without judgement from elders. Therefore, while being home in Naiyobi but away from his father was an emotional problem, it wasn't too much of a logistical problem. The logistical problem was in traveling back and forth between school and home.

Moshi, the town where Laizer's school was located, was a two-hundred-mile trip from Naiyobi. However, those weren't smooth miles traveled on paved highways in public buses. They included a twenty-five mile walk over plains with no roads from Naiyobi to Nainokanoka; a forty-five-mile ride in a crowded daladala on bumpy, unpaved roads from

Nainokanoka to Karatu; an eighty-five-mile ride in a crowded daladala on paved roads from Karatu to Arusha; and, finally, a fifty-mile ride in yet another crowded daladala from Arusha to Moshi.

The trip took between one and three days because there was only one daladala that ran between Nainokanoka and Karatu, which meant that there could be as much as a two-day wait for a ride. In addition to the logistical difficulty, each trip cost twenty-seven hundred shillings, which at the time equated to about three U.S. dollars. Neither Laizer nor his family had that much money; it would need to be paid by Laizer's sponsor. Each time, Laizer's sponsor sent it just in time for the trip—except for the one time when he didn't.

During Laizer's third year of school, his break came, but the money hadn't yet arrived. With school closing down and Laizer only having five hundred Tanzanian shillings, he had no choice but to walk home. He inquired about directions with a few students he thought might know the route. He learned that once he crossed the Monduli Mountains and the Engaruka plain, he would find three Maasai angan'gs where he could spend the night before making it the rest of the way to Naiyobi. It would be an arduous journey, but within the realm of trips he had taken as a warrior.

To prepare, Laizer changed into his orkarasha and beloved old tire shoes and went to the local market. He used his money to buy forty-five bananas for the trip. He ate three, put the rest into his backpack, and started walking. He brought no water. Not only did he have no way to carry it, but it wasn't even a consideration because Maasai rarely drink water. Out on the plains, water is hard to find and impossible to carry. Warriors train themselves to travel without water because they can't depend on it being available and can't let the lack of it prevent them from undertaking long, arduous journeys. Instead, the liquid obtained from any milk or blood they drink in the morning must sustain them throughout the day.

Once he left town, Laizer didn't use roads but followed a direct route, which decreased the distance from two hundred miles to around one hundred twenty-five miles. Since he was traveling through areas occupied by myriad dangerous animals, he had to limit his travel to daytime. Ol Doinyo Lengai was his north star; Laizer navigated his route by keeping the mountain in view. Although the days were foggy and cloudy, Ol Doinyo Lengai was visible across the wide-open plains.

The journey started out well. Laizer quickly left Moshi behind and entered the vast wilderness. Soon, he began to see zebras, monkeys, and antelopes of many kinds. Then it was secretary birds, wildebeests, and eland. Birds were everywhere. Thorny acacia trees dotted the landscape. As the day wore on, Laizer became increasingly uneasy as he saw buffaloes, elephants, and hyenas. He saw no lions, but he heard them. Well aware of the physical danger that he was in, Laizer was more than ready to get to safety.

Dusk had fallen by the time he arrived at the three angan'gs, and Laizer hurried inside. No one was there, so he entered the closest enkaji. He laid down just inside the doorway to sleep on the hard-packed earth, so he could periodically peer outside throughout the night. Although he had no flashlight, he could watch for approaching animals by moonlight and listen for their movements.

After a relatively sleepless night, Laizer arose at sunrise as he had many miles to go and wanted to take advantage of the daylight. He stepped outside the enkaji and peeled a twig from a Sodom apple shrub to brush his teeth. He surveyed the path ahead while brushing and watched as an enormous, ashy-brown python slithered out of the enkaji where he'd just spent the night, noiselessly meandering out into the plains without giving Laizer as much as a glance. Laizer stared at the track left in the dirt and shuddered—snakes frightened him more than lions.

Laizer shouldered his pack and started walking across the open plain in the direction of his home, with his toes hanging out the front of his tire shoes. The miles passed quickly, and he didn't stop to eat until early afternoon. By then, he was very hot and very hungry. When he opened his backpack, he found that some of the bananas were smashed. With over a hundred kilometers to go, having no water or other food, Laizer decided it would be best to eat the remainder of the bananas for energy before they were ruined. He sat and ate all forty-two of them.

These weren't full-sized bananas like what's typically found in American supermarkets, but they weren't the tiny ones, either. Being mushy, none of them tasted great, but they would serve his need for energy. It seemed like a reasonable decision at the time, so he choked them down and started walking again. At first, he merely felt full, but his stomach began to swell, and he struggled to continue walking. Within a few hours, his belly had expanded so much that he had to stop and lie down. Soon, he could not move at all. He couldn't vomit, pass gas, or defecate. Laizer's pain and discomfort were so intense he thought he might die.

Laizer started to search for a sharp root or stick that might puncture his stomach. Because of the agony, he didn't care that puncturing his abdomen would certainly result in his death—particularly in light of his current remoteness and isolation. The need for relief overtook all sense of logic or reasoning. Luckily, the minimal movement undertaken in search of an impalement device was exactly what he needed. His stomach soon started with some bubbling and gurgling and then moved on to enormous, airy burps.

Although the stench of his own burps was unbearable, the physical relief was immediate. As the gas rolled out of him, Laizer knew he was going to survive. Physically drained but able to continue, Laizer stood up to resume walking. Once upright, the floodgates opened, and a couple of kilograms of undigested banana shot out of his bowels as if erupting from Ol Doinyo Lengai.

Exhausted, mortified, and dehydrated, Laizer had no choice but to continue on his journey to the next angan'g. He arrived within hours and was able to rest, but due to the lost time, he was quickly back on his feet. Two days later, Laizer reached home. He immediately changed into his orkarasha and carefully tucked his pants, along with his pride, into his backpack until he could secretly wash them the following day. To this day, Laizer loathes the sight and smell of bananas. This was the only time the travel money didn't show up from his sponsor. During all the other trips between school and home, Laizer walked between Naiyobi and Nainokanoka and rode on daladalas for the rest of the journey.

Laizer increasingly wondered about his sponsor. Which one of the German tourists was he? Throughout primary school and for the first two years of secondary school, Laizer never knew. It wasn't until the third year of secondary school that Laizer finally started communicating with his sponsor. He did this through the help of a teacher who translated

Laizer's Swahili into his sponsor's English and vice versa—each of them writing in his second language. Laizer's sponsor wrote that he was thrilled to hear from Laizer, and Laizer was thrilled to connect with his sponsor. However, during Laizer's last year of high school, before he had a chance to email or call his sponsor directly, his sponsor suddenly died. The NCAA took on Laizer's sponsorship for that last year of high school and then sponsored him through college.

9

As NOTED EARLIER, THE MAASAI DIVIDE the males in their society into age-based cohorts to create rapidly mobilizable armies of warriors capable of serving broad geographic regions. To enter an age set, boys must be strong and brave, which is fundamental to the rigor, stamina, and stoicism of the warriors. This rite of passage is exciting, as warriors are respected and have a lot of freedom. Warriors form intense bonds of friendship and remain bonded in brotherhood for the rest of their lives. But inclusion in an age set doesn't come for free; each boy must earn it by facing one of the most sacred of Maasai rituals, called *emorata*, or ritual circumcision.

During the fall of Laizer's final year of secondary school, the Maasai's spiritual leader, called the Laiboni, started having dreams that portended coming change. He consulted with the tribal elders, and together they decided it was time for another age set to be created. To do this, they would open a season of emorata that December. During the next seven years, this ritual would be performed on boys in Maasai villages across northern Tanzania and southern Kenya. At the end of the seven years, these boys would form an age set.

They would train together and then defend their villages and cattle together as warriors.

If boys miss emorata during this seven-year period, they must wait another seven years until the Laiboni opens a new one. As such, some boys go through emorata at age twelve and others at age twenty. If a boy isn't ready, he can postpone his participation until the next emorata, but he won't be treated as a man until he is circumcised. Also, until he is circumcised, he can't spend time with those who have been circumcised.

During the season, there may be a total of twenty circumcisions performed each day, but they are spread across a wide geographic area. Once the circumcision season is closed after seven years, the thousands of Maasai boys who have been circumcised will comprise the new age set. Within a family, circumcision is traditionally completed in age order. As with marriage, the eldest son goes first and so on throughout the family. Each candidate for circumcision must be approved by his father and the tribal elders.

At eighteen years of age, Laizer was at the older end of eligible boys. The previous seven-year period had closed when he was eleven, and he had not been quite ready. After waiting another seven years for the next emorata to open, there was no question that he would participate. For Laizer, even having lived outside of the Maasai culture, this would be one of the most important days of his life. Rather than being afraid, he was anxious to get it done and embarrassed that he hadn't already had it done. He missed being with friends who were already circumcised, and he wanted the freedoms they had.

When Laizer came home from school in December, he told his father he was ready and wanted to be circumcised right away. Despite their tension, Mekuru was pleased. Yet

Mekuru needed to be sure Laizer was ready, for the consequences of failure are harsh not only for the one being circumcised, but for the whole family.

For the Maasai, circumcision is not just a procedure. It is a test of bravery, strength, and commitment. The circumciser, called the *alamoratani*, doesn't just cut the foreskin of the boy's penis. He makes ten cuts, including an incision along the length of the shaft. The procedure is done without any painkillers, using a knife that is only sharpened once, and with the entire village watching. A boy doesn't pass just by making it through the procedure without crying. To pass, he must not move at all, which includes twitching his eyelids, wiggling his toes, or moving in any outwardly detectable way. If a boy is successful in his circumcision, he enters the world of manhood and brings pride to his family.

While most boys do pass and become men, those who fail do so horribly. That moment can ruin their life. If a boy even twitches, he fails, but if a boy cries during circumcision, he loses the respect of others, is shunned, and lives on food scraps and waste for the rest of his life. Sometimes he is beaten so badly he is disfigured or killed. Sometimes the mothers are beaten along with their sons. The family banishes the boy and never speaks of him again. His failure brings shame to the whole family.

Laizer recalls seeing one boy crying during emorata. He was then beaten and later died from his injuries. He recalls another boy who cried and had to leave Naiyobi for the city, where he remains to this day. Laizer also speaks of an old man in his village who is still known as someone who cried during the cuts. It is also known to all the boys that the procedure can lead to life-threatening infections.

Laizer knew the risks, but he was ready, and he was persistent. His younger brothers were also anxious to go through emorata, but Laizer, as eldest, had to go first. With all his sons pestering him, Mekuru finally consented and decreed that Laizer's circumcision would occur when he came home from school during his June break. Two of his brothers would also be circumcised on that day. Mekuru indicated he would consider additional sons later during the seven-year circumcision "season," if they convinced him they were ready.

The day Laizer returned home from school in June, he began preparations for his emorata. Because he needed to provide honey beer to the elders, and the drink took a week or more to ferment, that was his first task. He then turned to preparing for the ceremony by ensuring he had enough ostrich feathers for his headdress. He had collected them during the rainy seasons of earlier years, as that was when the ostriches molted. It would now be time to use them. Finally, he cleaned his mother's angan'g and repaired her enkaji and then repaired his father's angan'g, as his father would be hosting the event.

Two days before Laizer's emorata, people started gathering. The elders drank the beer with Mekuru. The boys and their mothers made the final preparations. Laizer found an olive sapling and laid it down in front of his mother's enkaji. Laizer and his brothers sat on cowhides and teased each other as their mothers shaved the boys' heads. Shaving is done at each coming-of-age ritual to symbolize a new start. Additionally, the boys give away all their possessions to prepare for a new phase of life.

One day before, many more people arrived from around the village—Laizer remembers there being about eight hundred people present to watch the twenty boys get circumcised.

As was customary, some of them immediately started to harass Laizer and the other boys. The idea was to make the boys so angry that they would be able to withstand the pain. It started partway through the day when a large group of people took the boys' orkarashas. For the rest of the day, the boys were no longer allowed to enter their angan'gs and instead had to remain out in the open—naked and humiliated in front of everyone.

Villagers then chased them, spit at them, and taunted them. Even Laizer's beloved mother chased him with a big stick and told him that if he cried, she would die. She reminded him that no one in their family had ever cried and threatened him not to be the first. By night, Laizer was uncomfortable, ashamed of his nudity, and fuming at everyone. Hecklers then kept Laizer and the other boys awake throughout the night. By morning, Laizer was furious, and he was ready.

10

L AIZER, HIS BROTHERS LOSERIAN AND MELUBO, some
cousins, and friends totaled twenty. Twenty boys prepared to become men. Emotionally exhausted and angry in
their humiliation, they were ready for their trial. When the
Alamoratani decided it was time to begin, he called them
into Mekuru's angan'g. Inside the angan'g, each boy sat on a
cowhide in age order, with the oldest going first. Laizer was
the oldest in his family, but eleventh in the group.

It was so quiet the boys could hear their hearts beating.
Their bodies were pungent from nervous perspiration. Had
they lived near water, they would have left an axe in water
overnight to use the cold metal to numb themselves before the
procedure. Since they didn't, they would get nothing. They
waited in silence as the Alamoratani pulled out a knife and
knelt down in front of the oldest boy.

With the whole community watching, the Alamoratani
splashed the oldest boy's face with *enturoto*, a chalky mineral
mixed with milk or water, to make it more obvious if the boy
displayed any reaction. For the first boy, the knife was sharp,
and the cuts took only a few minutes. When he was done,

there was an audible sigh amongst the crowd, followed by cries of relief.

After the procedure is completed for each boy, he is allowed to cry out. In some cases, the boys work themselves into a hysterical ecstasy called *orkorio*, which involved screaming, yelling, flailing their arms, and thrashing around on the ground. The mental distraction and physical hyperventilation help alleviate the pain. Sometimes their mothers scream, yell, flail, and thrash along with their sons. After each boy's cutting is done, he becomes a man.

But there was no relief for those waiting with Laizer, and the wait felt interminable. By the time it was his turn, the once-sharp knife was dull and bloodied by the boys who had gone before him. It is customary for a trusted elder to hold each boy's back for support. For Laizer, the elder was supposed to be a brother-in-law, but he failed to appear until after Laizer's first few cuts. When the Alamoratani said, "First cut," Laizer braced himself. He had to start on his own. The Alamoratani's ritual took the pattern of cutting three times in a circle, then cutting the top, and finally pulling the skin back and cutting the tip.

The knife felt like a ragged chainsaw blade sawing back and forth. It was by far the worst pain Laizer had ever endured, but he sat rigid and kept staring straight ahead while the Alamoratani kept counting and cutting. After the cut on the tip, there was an incision along the length of his penis. It felt like it took ten or fifteen minutes—but who knows? Finally, Laizer heard the Alamoratani proclaim the number "ten," and the procedure was complete.

Naalamala, who witnessed the whole thing, now let her emotions flow. She cried and shook out her relief for herself and for her firstborn son. Through the throbbing pain, Laizer sat quietly, relief coursing through him as he waited for the rest of the boys to finish. The first of his brothers was third in line behind him, and his mother's cries of relief grew stronger as each son passed the test. In the end, the entire group made it through, and the community danced and sang with joy and relief.

Once all of the boys were cut, they were washed with cattle urine, which acted as an antiseptic but stung horribly. Laizer then went with his parents to receive a cow from his mother and a bull from his father. Afterward, he joined the other new recruits in a designated enkaji for a week of healing. They were fed blood mixed with liquid fat to help them heal, as well as *saroi*, which is fermented blood and milk, to help them rebuild their strength.

During this period of convalescence, called *osiplioli*, the men are treated like kings, even though they miss the party that immediately follows their circumcision. The celebration begins with their mothers planting the saplings they have collected in front of their enkajis, to symbolize success. That's quickly followed by a party, during which fathers proudly share meat with those in attendance. In Laizer's case, Mekuru killed three bulls, nine cows, and several goats for the party that lasted several days. As with Laizer's birth, this would be the second party in his honor that he wouldn't attend.

After a few weeks, the boys—who were now men—were healed. They emerged wearing the black clothes, bells, and white paint on their faces that is symbolic of those in the six-month post-circumcision period. In the past, the clothing had been made of cowhide, but by this time the clothing was usually made of black fabric. Newly circumcised men, energized with relief and newfound freedom, cannot be punished during this period. To celebrate their emergence, the men traditionally shoot wax-tipped arrows at girls who, in turn, give them gold rings. Laizer, who had been influenced by his schooling, didn't shoot the arrows at anyone but still received plenty of rings.

The men also shoot birds to make feathered headdresses and wear them as they travel from village to village, arriving just before the next group of boys is circumcised. Similar to the period before their emorata, the men taunt the boys and make them so angry that they won't cry from the pain when they are cut. As the men travel, they are fed by the local villagers. While this type of traveling celebration usually lasts for six months, Laizer only participated for a month because he had to wash off the paint, put on his uniform, and return to school.

By Laizer's December break from school, the six-month post-circumcision period was over. The rest of his group had now also washed off the black and white paint, discarded the headdresses, and replaced the black clothes with bright ork-arashas. Their mothers had again shaved their heads because the men were transitioning to junior warriors. Upon Laizer's return from school, his mother shaved his head, too, before he rejoined the others. The men would remain junior warriors until the seven-year circumcision season was over and the entire cohort of more than a thousand warriors was created. For Laizer, the full cohort would include eight of his brothers, as he was circumcised with two brothers and an additional six brothers were circumcised the following year. Thankfully, all of his friends and family made it through the ritual, but Laizer knows of three boys who bled to death during his seven-year circumcision season.

II

FINALLY, THE CIRCUMCISION SEASON ENDED, AND it was time to formally recognize the full age set as junior warriors at a ceremony called *imuget*. In this ceremony, each new warrior's head is again shaved by his mother, each warrior's family slaughters a cow, and all the tribes from many villages come to celebrate and eat. Based on the year in which Laizer was born, he would be part of what Americans call Generation X. In Maasailand, the fathers of Laizer's age set gave his cohort the name *Imirrishi*, meaning "unstoppable."

However, the age set just above Laizer's also gave his cohort a name, albeit a less-glamorous one: *Korianga*, meaning "honey badger." It was meant to be an insult referring to the badger's bad smell. Nicknaming is just one of the forms of hazing that keeps the younger cohort of junior warriors subordinate to the older cohort until many years later, when it is time for them to take the older cohort's place as full warriors.

The new warriors paint themselves with a mixture of ochre and animal fat and grow their hair long so they can braid it and twist in wool extensions. They adorn their earlobes, arms, necks, waists, and ankles with beaded ornaments made by girls and women. Their parents present them with the long spears that are the hallmark of the warrior. Warriors are never alone, and when they travel, they move across the plains in single file. It is at this point that Laizer's cohort took on the classic look of the Maasai and began the most adventurous years of their lives.

At first, warriors spend a few years training under the cohort above them. They develop strength and speed, learn to rapidly scale trees, practice using bush knives and throwing spears, and study how to care for an injured warrior. The warriors look after the cattle, vaccinate them, and keep them away from the seasonal wildebeests' migration path. The men perfect their skills in wildlife tracking and learn how to protect cattle from lions, cheetahs, and leopards while also learning how to protect themselves from those animals as well as the elephants and buffaloes. Essentially, they learn how to keep themselves, the others in their age set, and their cattle alive on the savannah among predators in the wilderness.

When Laizer's cohort went through training, their skills increased rapidly, and they were soon ready to take over for the older cohort. Although Laizer was only able to participate during breaks from school, he, too, was ready. Traditionally, the younger cohort challenges the older warriors and forces them to retire. This happens in a ceremony called Orng'esher. Like each ceremony that marks one of life's critical junctures, the warriors all have their heads shaved to leave the past behind and move into the next phase with a fresh start.

At the end of the ceremony, Laizer's cohort emerged as full warriors, with the full power to protect the community. As warriors, Laizer's age set lived apart from the community but was fully responsible for protecting it. While they wouldn't own any cattle, they would be responsible for the safety of the mature cattle owned by all members of the village. Functioning as a traveling brotherhood, their lives would be glamorous and exciting but also difficult and dangerous.

With their primary duty being the care of the cattle, the warriors' first priority was finding forage for cattle in all seasons. That could mean walking forty or more miles in one day to scope out potential grazing areas. In Naiyobi during the rainy season, Laizer and the other warriors herded cattle near Ol Doinyo Lengai, where the soil was salty and nourishing. During the dry season, they could stay closer to home. No matter how hot it was in the day or cold at night, the warriors were responsible for the protection of cattle at all times, which meant they even slept out with the cattle.

Being a warrior also meant being strong and quick, so they could assemble rapidly when summoned by the sound of the horn, which is taken from a greater kudu, which is a type of woodland antelope. In Mekuru's time, the Laiboni would occasionally call the warriors together and tell them it was time to go on a cattle raid. During Laizer's time, warriors were no longer summoned for raids but would respond to dangerous emergencies such as when lions had killed some of their cattle. To be nimble and travel far, warriors would carry only their spears. Not having reliable access to water, the warriors learned to travel without water or food. Instead, a cup of blood would sustain them for dozens of miles. Laizer never drank more than a few cups of blood in one sitting, but he had one brother who would drink up to three quarts in preparation for long journeys to find forage for the cattle.

To be prepared physically for long journeys and the dangers they would face, warriors were in continual practice.

Occasionally, they would even go on meat-eating retreats to bulk up and get ready. These retreats, called *orpuls*, are indulgences with a purpose—to prepare warriors for physically demanding work. Orpul gave warriors a chance to strengthen their bodies, their skills, their immunity, and their bonds of brotherhood. Laizer participated in orpul six times during his warrior years: two that he sponsored and four held by friends.

During orpul, a group of warriors travel far from their villages with their spears and cattle and don't return until all the cattle have been eaten. It can last weeks or even months. Once a camping spot is found, the party begins. The focus is to build strength, bond, and, in earlier times, emotionally prepare for a raid. They also drink bitter-tasting medicinal soups made from herbs and acacia bark to help them fight off parasites and boost their immune systems. Sickness not only threatens their survival, but it is also seen as a sign of weakness. The soup also makes them energetic, aggressive, and fearless, and it readies for challenges that traditionally range from cattle raids to fighting lions.

In addition to eating during -rpul, the warriors sing and dance. They practice standing jumps called *aigus*. Maasai are famous for these high jumps, which they achieve by never letting their heels touch the ground. They also engage in contests of skill and fitness, such as throwing spears and climbing trees. Once the party ends each night, the warriors sleep under the stars with just their orkarashas to keep them warm.

During these years, Laizer bonded with men more than with women due not only to having a cohort of brothers to train with, but also to strict warrior policies about staying away from women. The Maasai men believed being around women would weaken them. The warriors needed to be both physically strong to do their work and emotionally strong to cope with the loss of their brothers, although the high mortality rate among warriors mostly happened in the past, when they went on cattle raids. To prevent contamination from the women's perceived weakness, women were not even involved in any aspect of meal preparation for the warriors, including cooking, serving, or eating alongside the men. Only once the men retired from warriorhood and moved into the next phase of life—marriage and family—could they eat with women and children, typically their wives and offspring.

With warriors not being allowed to marry at this stage until recently, one might think they spent a lot of time dating young women, who would be especially attracted to the virile warriors. But Maasai warriors are only allowed to have sexual relations with uncircumcised girls, and since girls are circumcised right around puberty, their options are limited. By convention, girls are to leave warrior camps at the first sign of puberty to ensure that this rule is followed.

In practice, however, this rule leads to a lot of secret affairs. These affairs are detected at ceremonies when wives who have cheated on their husbands cannot shave their husbands' heads or remove their belts. At that time, the wife must pay the husband one of her cattle, and the warrior with whom she cheated must pay the husband ten of his. Children resulting from the affair remain the property of the husband and not the warrior.

Aside from potential fines, the warriors face very few consequences for their behavior. Although warriorhood is difficult, it is often the most exciting part of a Maasai man's life. The warriors are self-confident, supremely fit, and fearless.

They have a strong sense of purpose and an unbreakable bond with each other. Together, the warriors function as an army, tasked with the critical role of protecting the cattle and the entire Maasai community. But what about the women?

12

BY THE TIME LAIZER WAS CIRCUMCISED at age eighteen, two of his younger sisters had already been circumcised, married off, and had children. With so little communication between men and women, boys and men—especially unmarried ones—have little knowledge of what is happening in their sisters' lives, particularly with regard to circumcision, marriage, and motherhood. In fact, Laizer didn't know his sisters' stories until later in life and still doesn't know many of the details. When he did learn more about them, he was stunned.

As with boys, girls' rites of passage start with circumcision. But beyond that, there are few similarities. While men are circumcised to form an age set and serve as a cohort, women are circumcised to prepare for marriage. Circumcision for girls occurs at the first sign of puberty and is done alone or in a small group. There is no age-set cohort and no band of sisters with whom to bond and travel through life.

While there is some ceremony to female circumcision, it is nothing like the village-wide event culminating in massive celebrations for the boys. Instead, it is a more private affair, generally conducted in the doorway of the girl's mother's enkaji. To mentally prepare, some girls sing through the night prior to the cut. When it is time, they wear a belt of beads and hide their faces with white paint and beads. Many women gather to watch, but the only men allowed are the girl's father, her father's best friend, and the husband-to-be. The men who watch are front and center.

With her face painted white and covered in beads, the girl's fear is partly hidden when the circumciser, called the *Engamuratani*, kneels down in front of her. It is only after the Engamuratani starts cutting that the girl's fear and pain can no longer remain hidden. Since female circumcision is not a test of bravery, the girls are not shunned if they twitch or cry. Afterward, the wound is covered with leaves and the girl is left to begin her recovery while her father celebrates. After a night of excruciating pain, the Engamuratani checks to make sure the girl's clitoris and inner labia were completely removed. If any of the flesh remains, they cut it again.

The cut is purely traditional. It is done as a rite of passage to womanhood and prepares girls for marriage. It has no medical benefit. On the contrary, it causes many problems. The healing is slow, painful, and often incomplete, with some women suffering lifelong pain or other problems. Laizer knows five women who died from complications caused by their circumcisions. One bled to death that day. The other four developed infections and died soon after.

Perhaps the starkest difference in the men's and women's experiences is what happens after the healing. While a newly circumcised man begins his participation in a brotherhood of excitement and freedom, a newly circumcised woman remains alone until she is healed. Once healed, she is then married off to a man of her father's choosing. Sometimes the match is made as early as infancy. For the father of the girl, the arrangement is primarily a financial transaction, with a standard bridewealth consisting of five animals and one article each of tobacco, honey, and cloth. In former times, women were married to men who had already retired from warriorhood because warriors died too frequently to be husbands. That is less common today, since warriorhood is less risky and many warriors marry before they retire.

In some Maasai communities, alternate rituals have replaced circumcision. Some Maasai groups even openly speak out against the practice—including a celebrated Maasai men's cricket team from Kenya, named the Maasai Cricket Warriors. But these examples are the exception rather than the rule, tend to occur in communities already influenced by outside cultures, and are mostly in Kenya. In Tanzania, including Laizer's village of Naiyobi, where Maasai communities are often rural and less influenced by outside cultures, female circumcision is still almost universally performed. And since the government outlawed the practice in 1998, it is often happening to girls now at younger ages because families want to get their daughters cut before governments or schools intervene. Once circumcised, she is ready to be wed to a man of her father's choosing.

For the wedding, a bride's head is shaved, and she is anointed with lamb fat. Her mother gives her gourds that she will need in her new life for carrying milk and tea. Life as a wife will be difficult. She will build her family's home from mud, cattle dung, and sticks. Her home will be nestled within an angan'g among other relatives, although she will access it through her own gate. Whenever a warrior needs her enkaji, she will leave it without complaint. Tending children and milking animals, fetching water and wood, brewing tea, beading, building homes, milking the cows, and laundry will make up the essence of her daily life.

Only after she has children—especially sons—will she have any status. She will love her children and have especially strong bonds with her sons, but she will not have control over her own children. Because she loves her children and does not want to lose contact with them, she is left in a challenging situation. She now must do whatever her husband commands, and he can beat her without recourse. Although she can divorce, if she does, she will never be allowed to remarry, and she will lose her children—even if they are fathered by someone else. She has no cohort, no freedom, and no control over her own life.

13

During Laizer's warrior years, he moved back and forth between warriorhood and college, which meant shifting everything from his language to his clothing, diet, and lifestyle. Awkward at first, he learned to make the transition fluidly and would look forward to the change of pace. Ideally, Laizer would have studied politics in college since he either wanted to go into politics or be a tour guide. However, at the time he entered college, a Danish group had given the NCAA a large grant to buy cattle for the Maasai and to sponsor students in veterinary science to enable them to treat their own cattle. As such, Laizer became the first person from Naiyobi ever to go to college, and he did it on a full scholarship.

In college, Laizer again had a mattress, but now he even had his own room. His food also improved again—this time it came without the maggots and with a side of rice. College ran from September through July for three years. Laizer's coursework included traditional classroom studies and valuable field studies throughout Tanzania, which allowed the students to visit veterinary projects and learn from rangers who were out treating animals in a variety of conditions. Laizer loved it. The experiences continued to expose him to the outer world.

Although Laizer had classes and a Saturday job, he still had more freedom than ever before and more time to spend with friends. He spent a lot of time with Julius, his friend from secondary school. Laizer still laughs at the sweet memory of the school's monthly parties, where the students would dance to disco music. He also spent some time noticing the women in his classes, such as Gracie, who had grown up in the town of Monduli. Monduli was more developed than Naiyobi, and it was more common for girls from that town to attend school, especially those from the wealthier families such as Gracie's, who could afford their children's schooling.

Gracie must have been noticing Laizer as well because one Saturday she offered to wash his clothes. He accepted and afterward sent her a letter to thank her. The following Saturday, Gracie made the same offer. This time, Laizer paid for the soap, and a friendship began. Gracie was a short, quiet woman, and Laizers says they both enjoyed spending time talking about life and what the future might be like.

When he was back in Naiyobi during one August break from college, Laizer told his father that he was in love with Gracie and wanted to marry her. Mekuru was enraged. He stared into Laizer's eyes and reminded him that, long ago, he had paid a bridewealth of nine cattle to a trusted friend to ensure their children would marry. He would not hear that his firstborn son would betray this arrangement. Maasai sons simply did not say no to their fathers. It upset the order of things. But once again, Laizer stood firm. It was several days until Mekuru cooled back down.

After Laizer's declaration of his intention to marry Gracie, Mekuru finally accepted that he couldn't force Laizer into an arranged marriage. Mekuru could, however, force Laizer to pay for the damage his refusal did to the natural order of things. Although Loserian, Laizer's next oldest brother, agreed to take on the marriage, as firstborn son, Laizer should have been the first to marry. To avoid any bad luck Laizer might cause by upsetting the family's birth order for marriage, Mekuru required his son to pay him one cow. Laizer agreed.

When Laizer returned to school in September, he talked to Gracie about marriage. He told her that at the end of his three years in college, he would complete his warriorhood and work to earn the nine cattle he would need to pay Gracie's father so that he could marry her. After that, Laizer would travel to her village of Monduli, and they would marry. While they were apart, they would have no way to communicate directly. The only way Laizer could contact Gracie during that time was by using the radio at the ranger station that had been built in Naiyobi to call the police station in her town.

What they expected to be a brief separation became eight months long as Laizer raised the funds to buy the cattle. Meanwhile, Mekuru continued trying to talk Laizer into going through with his previously arranged marriage. Laizer remained stalwart in his desire to marry Gracie and didn't budge or bend to Mekuru's will.

Finally, Laizer could afford the nine cattle, and Laizer's uncle, Ole-Ngolenya, agreed to walk to Monduli with him so he could see Gracie. As is customary when Maasai travel, they shortened the one hundred forty-five miles it would have taken by road by about half by going directly through the plains. It took them three days to walk to Monduli. When

Laizer and Ole-Ngolenya arrived in Gracie's village, Gracie was shocked to see Laizer. After not hearing from him for so long, she had found another boyfriend and was already pregnant. Devastated, Laizer and his uncle could do nothing but turn around and walk for three days back home.

Upon their return to Naiyobi, Mekuru, who at the time had five wives, gloated.

"You see?" he said. "This is why we have arranged marriages. You are playing around like a young child."

But rather than agreeing to the arranged marriage, Laizer decided he no longer wanted to be married at all—a bigger blow to Mekuru than Laizer's wanting to marry Gracie.

Mekuru never spoke about how he felt when his son was influenced by the outside world and betrayed him by going against the Maasai ways. And Mekuru didn't talk about how he felt when the outside world started to encroach upon his beloved hometown, upsetting what was familiar. First the school, then the church, next the ranger station, and soon there would even be an unmaintained, bumpy dirt road. Mekuru just stewed, drank, and lashed out at whoever was near who would not fight back. He held on tightly to his traditions, which provided order in the increasingly chaotic world around him. Laizer, meanwhile, grew despondent.

A few years later, Loserian took on the arranged marriage of Laizer's lifelong betrothed. As promised, Laizer paid his brother one cow for the penalty of not marrying in birth order, but he did not attend the wedding.

14

During the years Laizer was at school, he wore western-style clothes and focused on his studies. Over breaks, he would return to his village of Naiyobi, pack away his western clothing, put on his orkarasha and a pair of rubber tire shoes, and embrace his life as a Maasai warrior. In Naiyobi, school was far from his mind, as warriorhood took all his concentration. Warriors need to be ready for anything, including being face to face with a lion.

It is often said that Maasai men are each required to kill a lion during their warrior years. That isn't true, nor is it even possible; there simply aren't enough lions in East Africa. However, Maasai warriors who do kill lions gain great respect. Today, African lions are protected in Tanzania, and Laizer is very much in favor of their protection. But that wasn't the case during his warrior days. Back then, the proper response to a lion that preyed on Maasai livestock was to kill it.

When Maasai warriors headed out to kill a lion, their objective wasn't simply to take its life; their objective was to win the battle with the lion. To do so, a warrior, armed with only a spear, has to kill the lion without being injured himself.

If the warrior is injured, the lion wins. Since lions don't run away when speared but instead stay and fight, killing one of these incredible creatures is a difficult proposition. When multiple warriors spear a lion, they fight to determine who gets to claim victory. Each warrior not only has to fight the lion, but also his age mates. Since lions are a symbol of bravery and pride, a warrior who kills a lion is respected by everyone. Family and age-set allegiances are secondary to a chance for a personal win.

Laizer's father, Mekuru, had won respect for facing one lion and killing another during his warrior days. Once, a lion came to orpul, and Mekuru put meat on a spear and fed it. Another time, Mekuru went to battle with a lion and won. Laizer doesn't know if his father had been the one to actually kill that lion or if Mekuru had simply won a fight with an age mate who had done the killing. Nonetheless, Mekuru became a sought-after husband. But Mekuru's brave feats didn't provide Laizer with any inherited privilege. Maasai have a saying: "Even a lion can give birth to a hyena." If Laizer wanted respect, he would have to earn it himself.

Laizer's first experience with a lion hunt was during his time as a junior warrior. After a lion entered an angan'g to kill a cow, a group of eighty warriors left in pursuit of the lion. About forty warriors tried to get ahead of the lion, while the other half stayed back to track its movements. Laizer was in the first group.

Unexpectedly, it was the second group that came upon the lion, which was so large that they first thought it was an eland, the world's largest antelope. But then it started to vomit up its food, which is what lions do when they have just eaten and are preparing for a fight. The group was split as to the appropriate strategy. Some wanted to run right in and kill it, and others wanted to wait until the lion finished regurgitating to make for a better fight. They decided to wait for the lion to become ready, then run directly at it.

The fastest runner should have had the best chance to spear the lion, but he tired himself out on the run. When he threw his spear, he didn't have enough power behind it, and it merely injured the lion. The animal jumped up, grabbed the warrior, and tucked him under his body. When the other warriors arrived, they were afraid to try and spear the lion because they feared accidentally spearing the warrior. Instead, they circled the cat while yelling to the captured warrior to play dead. Finally, one warrior moved in to try to spear the lion. When the animal turned to react, his prisoner attempted to get away, so it used its jaws to grab the warrior near his shoulder blade and shook him, which ripped him open.

At that point, all the warriors jumped in and speared the lion. Finally, someone killed it with a bush knife. The warriors then grabbed the injured warrior. By a stroke of luck, a safari vehicle was nearby, and the driver loaded the warrior in with the stunned vacationers to take him to the hospital. The injured warrior survived but suffered paralysis in the injured arm. The lion had won.

Several years later, Laizer was on his second lion hunt. Once again, a lion had entered a village angan'g. This time, the lion jumped the acacia fence and killed three cows. When the women in the angan'g yelled, the lion left without the cows because it couldn't escape back over the fence with them. The women quickly alerted the local warriors, one of whom blew the greater kudu horn to round up their cohort to pursue the lion.

When the call went out, Laizer was heading into the village, but he was still too far out to hear it. When he arrived holding his spear and looking for his age mates, some women asked why he hadn't gone. When he innocently asked, "Gone where?" the women explained about the lion, and Laizer, embarrassed to have missed the call, grabbed his spear and ran to catch up. Soon, he spotted about sixty warriors in the distance, and he yelled to them that he was coming. When the other warriors turned, they saw what they were looking for and yelled back, "The lion is right near you!"

At first, Laizer didn't see the lion; he was looking too far into the distance. Then, as his focus shifted closer, he not only saw it, but he smelled it. The lion was crouched down in the grass fewer than ten yards away. Laizer's heart thumped as he backed up about two yards. He considered running, but he knew that would not only cause him great humiliation but also death because the lion would chase him and kill him. So, instead, he froze and watched as the lion stood and stalked him, its face covered in cow blood, its eyes staring intently at him.

Laizer shook as he raised his spear, waiting for the other warriors to arrive. He never took his eyes off the lion. Suddenly, the giant cat lunged into the air, and Laizer reacted instinctively. His spear flew straight, hitting the animal in the head with such force that it came out through the back of the skull. Full of adrenaline, Laizer no longer stood his ground. He turned and ran about twenty yards before he realized the lion wasn't after him. It must have died immediately; it lay still in the grass.

Minutes later, Laizer's friends showed up, embraced him, and offered congratulations and adulation. There was no doubt about who had made this kill. Laizer cut off the lion's tail and attached it to the end of his spear. For the next three days, the warriors celebrated. Laizer led a huge procession of hundreds of warriors through local villages, where local women gave them milk and blessings. Even Laizer's father congratulated him and celebrated by sharing more details about his own lion kills than he ever had before. Laizer had earned respect, credibility, and a voice among the Maasai.

Soon after, he was back in western clothes and starting the next semester of college.

Laizer's enkaji in Naiyobi, Tanzania, in 2014. Credit: Kim Laizer

*Laizer with friends Noel, Simon, and Omary at Simanjiro College in
2000. Credit: Jeremia (last name unknown)*

Olotumi Laizer, Kim Laizer, Mekuru Laizer, and Naalamala Laizer
in Naiyobi, Tanzania, in 2009. Credit: Kim Laizer

The first Yosemite group to visit Tanzania with Laizer and Kim at
Olmolti Crater in 2014. Credit: Kim Laizer

The Serengeti ecosystem is famous for the wildebeest and zebra migration, seen here in 2016. Credit: Rachel Mazur

Laizer with two of his mothers, Naatemuta (Laizer's right) and Naalamala, in Naiyobi, Tanzania, in 2014. Credit: Kim Laizer

Laizer distributing rice to his family while visiting his home in Naiyobi, Tanzania, in 2016. Credit: Kim Laizer

Laizer and Kim (fifth and sixth adults standing, from left) with several family members in Naiyobi, Tanzania, in 2016. Credit: Rachel Mazur

A Yosemite group shopping at a makeshift jewelry market in front of Ol Doinyo Lengai in Naiyobi, Tanzania, in 2014.
Credit: Winston Seiler

Mekuru Laizer (squatting with hat) with four of his wives and their children in Naiyobi, Tanzania, in 2016. Credit: Kim Laizer

An African (cape) buffalo stands in front of a group of wildebeests at the edge of Naiyobi, Tanzania, in 2016. Credit: Rachel Mazur

Laizer at Yosemite National Park, California, in 2019. Credit: Kim Laizer

Theresia Julius Saruni and Kim Laizer (third and fourth from left in front row) with women participating in Nadupoi programs in Naiyobi, Tanzania, in 2018. Credit: Kim Laizer

Magdelena Yohana (bottom, left) teaching local women through a Nadupoi program in Naiyobi, Tanzania, in 2017. Credit: Kim Laizer

Laizer and his father, Mekuru, in front of the ranger station in Naiyobi, Tanzania, in 2021. Credit: Kim Laizer

Laizer with students whom he and friends sponsored in Nainokanoka, Tanzania, in 2017. Credit: Olotumi Laizer

15

Most of Laizer's time as a warrior was much less exhilarating than facing lions. In fact, one of his major tasks was watering the cattle. With limited access to water, watering the cattle could be time consuming, not to mention contentious. During the dry season, water is so scarce that warriors have to wait in line for it. Laizer recalls a time when he was the seventh person in line with about thirty cattle. The eleventh person in line took his own twenty cattle to the front. When Laizer tried to push past him, the other warrior started to beat Laizer's cattle, so Laizer had to fight with him to keep his place in line.

Fights are one way that warriors challenge each other to gain status. Those who can't fight lose their ability to defend their family and their animals. Sometimes fights escalate, and for that reason the elders select individuals from the warrior age set to serve as chiefs to solve problems. It is an appointed role one cannot turn down. One of Laizer's friends was selected for chief of his warrior age set. While the chiefs get some privileges, such as spending time with the elders and being allowed to marry early, their responsibilities negotiating with the elders cause them to miss out on a lot of warrior adventures.

And warriors do have a lot of adventures, both exciting and ill-conceived. The year after Laizer won the fight with the lion, he was watching buffaloes with a group of warriors when one said, "Who is brave enough to feed a buffalo?" Knowing how dangerous buffaloes are but wanting to appear brave, Laizer volunteered. He prepared by taking off his clothes and then rubbing mud all over his naked body to mask his human smell. Laizer then sneaked around the bushes where a buffalo was eating and held out grass to it.

He fed the buffalo safely twice, but on the third attempt, the buffalo started to chase him, saliva spewing from its mouth and nose. Laizer's speed and warrior tree-climbing skills were no match for the buffalo, so he had to fight it off with a machete. Laizer's friends, who were laughing the whole time at this comedic episode from their safe perch on the hillside, came and helped him fend off the buffalo.

Another time, Laizer was out on the savannah with some warriors searching for lost cattle. As a group traveling across the landscape, the Maasai warriors always move in a single-file line, maintaining about fifteen yards of separation between each warrior so as not to startle or spear each other. On this occasion, they were moving along a narrow, bushy trail with poor visibility. Suddenly, the warrior just ahead of Laizer startled a buffalo that was sleeping in the middle of the trail.

The buffalo tried to attack him, so he retreated, running at full speed past Laizer. This commotion caused Laizer to trip on a thick vine and drive his spear through his lower thigh, dislodging his patella. Laizer pulled the spear back out and walked roughly a mile back toward the village before collapsing. The other warriors carried him the rest of the way home.

After a week recuperating, Laizer had such a dangerous wound infection that his friends gave him antibiotics meant for cattle. With neither a hospital nor a doctor in town, they had to try what they could to save him. A day later, his leg and stomach started swelling. Mekuru wanted to wait it out, but Laizer's uncle, Melani, said, "No, Laizer must go to the hospital," and loaned Mekuru money to send Lazier to the hospital in Karatu. Loserian also went. The doctor remarked that Laizer had been within a day of losing his leg and then his life. While Laizer didn't lose either, the injury effectively ended his time on the Tanzanian soccer team.

16

WHEN LAIZER FINISHED COLLEGE, HE IMMEDIATELY started working as a veterinarian. His job included advising people on animal care, providing animal vaccinations, examining cattle to determine whether their meat was safe to go to market, and reporting any livestock diseases to the government. As an employee of the Tanzanian government, Laizer received free housing but had no choice in where he was assigned.

His first location in this position was in southern Tanzania near Mozambique. This placed Laizer a long distance from his family, and he didn't earn enough money or have enough time off to visit home, though he saved as much as he could. Despite the tension with his father, he was homesick. He missed the big open plains, his mother's quiet companionship, and his friends surrounding him. After his requests to move farther north went unanswered for a year, Laizer used the money he had saved to buy his mother eight cattle, which immediately increased her ability to feed her family as well as her status, and then he quit his job.

Back home, Laizer used his veterinary knowledge to start a small veterinary supply store in Naiyobi until he could figure out what to do next. Laizer was glad to be back in Naiyobi and wanted to settle nearby, but not so close as to be dominated by Mekuru. To find a professional job, Laizer needed retraining. He decided to ask the NCAA to sponsor him to return to college for a second degree. As a wildlife agency, the NCAA was willing to sponsor Laizer to seek a degree in wildlife management, which would prepare him to work in the NCA as a wildlife biologist.

This time, Laizer was able to dive right into his studies. Being back at school and studying science, he started to further question some of the Maasai beliefs and traditions he had learned from his father. For example, he learned that Nemulo, the half-metal/half-human animal he'd been taught to fear, didn't exist. When he was home over breaks, Laizer shared this information with his family, but they didn't believe him. Not only did they insist that Nemulo was real, but Ole-Ngolenya even insisted he had seen it with his own eyes during an orpul. Laizer also learned about the ecology of lions. He studied the lion's role in the ecosystem and the threats to their survival, including killings by the Maasai, and became protective of them.

Pursuing a second degree paid off. Within a year, Laizer found a job as a safari guide, which he could do during school breaks. The salary, particularly the tips, amounted to more money than Laizer had ever had before. He was experiencing another first in a life full of firsts. Now every time Laizer went home, he was able to bring food for the whole family and clothes for the children. And, ironically, with this contribution from working with non-Maasai foreigners, Laizer started to win back the favor of Mekuru, who wanted nothing to do with the outside world. Mekuru began boasting, "Laizer is a good man, and he has a big heart," to whoever would listen.

Meanwhile, the whole experience of guiding safaris continued to provide Laizer with experiences and relationships that affected his worldview. Laizer initially guided tourists on driving tours through wildlife parks and on walking treks up Mount Kilimanjaro, located right near his college in Moshi. In this line of work, he often collaborated with his brother Emanuel, who was now also studying wildlife management.

While Laizer now had much more experience with non-Maasai people than when the German tourists had stopped him as a young boy herding goats, he still had little experience with wealthy foreigners. In Tanzania, which is home to more than one hundred twenty-five distinct ethnic groups, ninety-nine percent of residents are from within Africa, and the majority or residents live in poverty.

In contrast, well over ninety-nine percent of Laizer's safari clients were from Europe, Australia, and the United States; were generally very wealthy; and were predominantly white. Prior to working for the safari company, the only white person Laizer had spent time with was Ned, the pastor who had befriended him in primary school. Otherwise, he knew only what his father had told him about whites and other wealthy foreigners—that they had come to Tanzania to take control, but they would never take control of the Maasai.

Being suddenly in the business of catering to wealthy clients for multiple days at a time was eye-opening. Laizer had assumed he'd learned a passable level of English in college. But when in the presence of a group of English speakers, he could hardly understand what they were saying. They spoke quickly with many accents, and they used slang terms he'd never learned.

Laizer was also faced with the stark differences between the life he lived and the way the visitors expected to be treated. For one, Laizer had been hungry most of his life and had learned never to waste food. The visitors had a surplus of food and threw out much of it. For another, Laizer had grown up with a zero-waste attitude. With the exception of a few metal utensils, a bowl, a water jug, and an orkarasha, everything a Maasai owned was compostable. In stark contrast, the safari visitors generated a lot of waste—from plastic wrappings to the use of fossil fuels.

Most of the visitors seemed oblivious to these differences. They would fly in from all around the world, drive all over Tanzania, stay at elaborate safari lodges, photograph the locals and the wildlife, and leave. In the process, they would emit more carbon, use more water, and leave more waste than most Maasai produce in a lifetime. Perhaps they would be generous and dole out pencils or candy to the children. While doing this, some would stand in the safari jeep and chat about how the Maasai were hard on the environment because they kept cattle. As their guide, all Laizer could do was listen and shake his head.

There were also aspects of safety that felt inconsistent to Laizer. As a warrior, Laizer spent years out in the plains, armed only with a spear. With safari groups, he traveled through the plains in an armored vehicle for safety and left the parks just before dark, as was required of safari guides. And while the safari groups generally stuck to the vehicles for safety as they were advised, there were often tourists who wouldn't heed Laizer's advice in other situations.

Laizer remembers one tourist who dragged him along to climb an active volcano and stay at the top for seven days to film it. When Laizer warned him of the dangerous places where he should not sit or leave his belongings, the man scoffed, "I'm a geologist, and I know how to be safe here." In the end, the tourist lost four cameras to the lava and cried on the way down. Blaming Laizer for his loss, he didn't even leave a tip.

Regardless, safety was paramount when hosting groups of wealthy travelers. One time when they had just arrived at a camp, Laizer and Emanuel gathered a new group to instruct them in camp safety. Emanuel gave a presentation emphasizing that they were in the Serengeti, where many creatures, from insects to black mambas, lived, and that they should be kept out of the tents. He cautioned that they should plan to each take a friend or guide with them when they went to the bathroom, to be safe.

He further explained that, as they walked, they should have their lights on, but if they saw an animal, they should immediately shut the lights off and walk back to relieve themselves near the tent instead. Elephants and buffaloes don't like lights and would therefore come straight at the tourists holding them, whereas if they flashed a light at a lion, it would just lie down. He closed with the main point of his lecture, which was that when the travelers left their tents, they must zip them closed.

The next day, the group went on a morning game drive, then returned to have lunch and relax before going out again for an evening game drive. During the afternoon break, Emanuel went into his tent to grab his shower kit, but he neglected to close his tent. When he returned, he got back into his tent, zipped it closed, and took out his clean clothes. As he was pushing his sleeping bag to the side to make room to get dressed, a cobra slithered out of it. When Emanuel frantically shouted, "Snake, snake, snake!" and jumped around in his tent, everyone from the group as well as from the other safari groups who were camping nearby gathered around. Laizer tried to calm him to get him to stop moving, but he was frantic.

Finally, Laizer took a knife and cut the tent open to get his brother out. Emanuel ran out completely naked, followed quickly by the cobra. The snake was aggressively approaching people, so Laizer swiftly killed it. He then turned to Emanuel and saw that he was still stark naked and in a panic. No one in the crowd had even given Emanuel a towel to cover his body—they were too busy gawking and taking pictures of the naked Maasai man.

Laizer quickly found something to wrap his brother in and asked if he had been bitten. Emanuel said yes, so they acted immediately. Knowing one can die from a cobra bite within an hour and that it would take almost four hours to get to the nearest hospital in Karatu, Laizer and a third guide hustled Emanuel into one of the jeeps and sped off. Fortunately, despite the usual herds of gazelles crossing the road, they didn't hit any animals, likely because the rough dirt road didn't allow them to go as fast as they would have liked.

After about forty-five minutes of driving, the other guide said to Laizer's brother, "You seem normal. Are you sure you were bitten?" Emanuel, who was still frantic, responded, "I don't know for sure, but I must have been after being with it in that tent." At that point, Laizer's friend, who was driving, stopped the car. "You don't know?" he asked. Since Emanuel seemed healthy, had no pain, and didn't really know where he had been bitten, Laizer and the other guide started examining him.

They determined that there was no way he could have been bitten without a mark and with no visible sign of a reaction. Then they sat for a while to decide what to do. Emanuel was too embarrassed to go back to the safari camp, but there didn't seem to be any reason to continue to Karatu, especially since the roundtrip would take all day and they were still in charge of the group of visitors back at camp.

They finally turned and drove slowly back, even more slowly than they normally would on those rough roads. When they finally returned to the group, Laizer's brother laid down in his seat to hide. What struck Laizer was the faces of the group members, who were distraught and assumed the worst. But then the driver got out smiling, and Laizer got out laughing, and, a few minutes later, Emanuel crawled sheepishly out of the backseat. When Laizer told the group what had happened, everyone fell down laughing so hard that, finally, even Emanuel was laughing. It was all the group talked about for the rest of the night.

Later, some people in the group told Laizer that since they couldn't see Emanuel when the jeep had pulled up, they had thought he had died and wondered if Laizer and the other guide had left his body out on the plains. Others told Laizer they'd thought he and the other guide had put Emanuel's dead body in the back of the Jeep but had only returned to tell the group they were going to go put his body out somewhere.

Laizer only laughed in response, but silently he thought back to the day when he and his friends had come upon a dead man's remains. What would the man have wanted done with his remains? Leave them to compost back to the natural world, or put them in a metal box, where they would forever impose upon the natural world like the many wrappers and trappings of the tourists?

The tourists' questions about what the Maasai did with their dead weren't offensive, but the way they asked such questions was sometimes difficult. It sometimes felt more like ridicule than honest curiosity. As a guide with limited knowledge of English, Laizer had to hold his tongue on many occasions. Sometimes their comments were due to obliviousness, such as when they wondered aloud how people could live a certain way, as if it was always their choice, when it was obviously linked to poverty. Other times it was from a lack of empathy, such as noting how quaint it was that women walked such great distances while carrying water on their heads. The comments could also just be plain rude, such as when tourists mocked the Maasai despite knowing their guide was from that same culture. Few visitors ever considered that their guides could also be malnourished, suffering from malaria, or worried about sick family members.

Thankfully, that wasn't true of all visitors. Many were curious, empathetic, and kind. This was particularly true of an American woman named Kim, who came to Tanzania in 2008 to fulfill a dream of learning about the wildlife and the cultures of Tanzania, and who had no idea Tanzania would soon become central to her life.

17

EARLIER THAT YEAR, KIM HAD STARTED dreaming about taking a trip to Tanzania to experience its wildebeest migration, music, and culture. As an environmental educator at the Yosemite Institute (YI) in California in the United States, she was eligible to apply for a Matthew A. Baxter III Memorial Award. In her application, Kim described wanting to learn about the country's "rhythms of life" and to spend time volunteering to help build a house for a family, for which she'd spent time raising funds. She received the award.

Matthew Baxter was an enthusiastic, adventurous, compassionate man who fell to his death while climbing El Capitan at Yosemite National Park in 1996. At the time, Mathew had been working for YI, and the following year, YI created the Baxter Award to provide up to three YI (now called NatureBridge) employees each year with the finances and time to experiment with a personal challenge. Baxter recipients have traveled all around the world and helped with a myriad of causes.

That same year, Kim also received a Bishop Marcus Award, which honors the memories of Drs. Barry C.

Bishop and Melvin G. Marcus, both YI environmental educators and members of its board. These two men valued environmental education, fun, adventure, and good will. Like the Baxter Award, this financial award encourages professional development of environmental educators by encouraging them to take on personal challenges. With the combined funds from these two awards, Kim planned a full ten-week experience.

As part of Kim's trip to Tanzania, she participated in the Aang Serian Cultural Summer School Program, hosted by a company called Oreteti, which happened to be the company that employed Laizer. Kim and six other women from the U.S., Canada, and England would spend three weeks together throughout the program. During each of the three weeks, the group would learn about a different Tanzanian tribe through immersion and cultural instruction. The first week of the program was about Chaga culture. During that week, the group's primary guide was from the Chaga tribe, but other Oreteti employees were around to help out as well. That week, Kim met Laizer and practiced Swahili a bit with him but otherwise didn't spend much time with him. The second week, however, was about Maasai culture, and Laizer was the group's guide.

For the Maasai week, the immersion experience included everything from learning about jewelry-making to watching their hosts puncture a bull's neck and drink its blood. They entered an angan'g and got to see the inside of the enkajis, hear the Maasai women sing, and even watch the warriors slaughter a goat for orpul. By now, Laizer was used to the jokes from tourists, and when the expected quips about the Maasai culture came along, they didn't bother him.

This time, however, he noticed that Kim didn't laugh along with the others. Instead, she stood up for the Maasai and gently urged the others to consider their cultural bias. Laizer also noticed Kim was a little quieter than the others and more introspective. Laizer doesn't know how or why it happened, but very quickly, he found he had fallen in love.

At the end of the week of cultural learning about the Maasai, the group spent two days installing an underground water tank for a local school. During one break, Laizer and Kim walked together to a hilltop to take some photos. While there, Kim told Laizer she wanted to climb Mount Kilimanjaro. Laizer suggested she book a hike through Oreteti. Although he'd recently told his boss he no longer wanted to guide trips up Mount Kilimanjaro, he hoped he could accompany her on the trip. During the last week of the immersion—which was about the Hadzabe tribe—Kim took Laizer's advice and signed up to go on the trek to climb the mountain the following week.

Laizer appealed to his boss to let him go on the trip, but she said no. She needed him for a high-profile group going to the Serengeti. But Laizer was persistent, so his boss finally agreed that he could go, but only as a volunteer, meaning that he would only receive food as compensation. Laizer agreed. The staffing for the trip therefore included the paid guide, two porters, a cook, and Laizer. As they hiked up the mountain, the paid guide led the way, but Laizer walked with Kim, talking with her about life and explaining what they saw along the way. Since Kim didn't know Laizer was only a volunteer on the trip, it made sense to her that he would do that.

A few days into the trip, one of the porters became ill and had to hike out. The porter took one of the three tents with him, leaving only one tent for Laizer, the guide, the cook, and the remaining porter to all share, and a second tent just for Kim, who was the only client on the trip. Kim offered to share with Laizer, but Laizer refused. He was worried that if he showed any feelings toward her, she would get angry and that would result in his getting fired.

For the full seven days of the trip, Laizer enjoyed Kim's company while hiding his true feelings. Even when, on the very last night of the trip, Laizer invited Kim to visit his family in Naiyobi, he did so under the guise of giving her experiences. Unfortunately, she already had plans to go to Zanzibar. At the end of the hike up Mount Kilimanjaro, the group returned to Arusha, where Kim tipped out each of the employees, including forty dollars to Laizer.

Kim invited Laizer to go out for pizza on her last night in Arusha before she left for Zanzibar, but this time it was Laizer who already had plans. In the end, Laizer and Kim were able to spend time together later that evening, but in the company of others as well. When Kim did buy Laizer a pizza, he shared it with everyone present, which is the traditional way with Maasai, and had little more than a bite for himself. It wasn't enough—not of the pizza, but of the time with Kim. Laizer was desperate to see her again before she left for what seemed like the other end of the earth, so he offered to take her to the airport when she returned to Arusha from Zanzibar.

In the days she was gone, Laizer met up with the guide who had led the Serengeti trip in his place. Laizer told him about his time with Kim, and the other guide laughed and bragged about his tip, which included one thousand dollars, a camera, and a nice pair of shoes. He mocked Laizer for giving all that up for "forty dollars and a bite of Kim's pizza." But

Laizer just smiled. He hadn't been looking for money. He had been looking for time with Kim. He spent the days while she was gone longing for her and confiding in his friends about this girl from across the world who had stolen his heart.

When Kim returned from Zanzibar, Laizer was waiting at the hotel where Kim had stored her large backpack so she could travel light to Zanzibar.

"Laizer, you're here!" Kim's eyes lit up and she smiled broadly when she saw him waiting.

"Yes, I am here," he responded. He smiled back, but then stopped as he quickly added, "I wanted to make sure you could get to the airport."

"Are you sure you didn't just want to see me again?" Kim teased.

Laizer tried looking away, but it was hard not to keep glancing back at her radiant smile.

"Well, I am so happy to see you," Kim said. "And I will gladly take you up on the trip to the airport. But since I have some time, let's have some lunch first."

Laizer and Kim sat down for a simple lunch in the outdoor area at the hotel. Other diners came and went, were too engrossed in each other's stories to notice, until Laizer abruptly noted, "We need to get to the airport."

Kim paid their check while Laizer made arrangements for a ride to the airport, and they were quickly on their way. As they sat together, their hands were close, but Laizer made sure they didn't touch. His attraction to Kim was second only to his fear of the potential repercussions of an unwanted advance.

There was little traffic, and they easily made it in time. Although the Arusha airport is small and doesn't host many flights, the line to check in was slow and the air was hot and stagnant. As Kim stood in line, she frequently glanced over at Laizer, whose expression betrayed no emotion as he waited patiently nearby.

Once Kim was checked in, she walked back over to Laizer.

"I'm all checked in and just have to go through security," she said, then turned silent and gazed at Laizer, giving him the space to say what was on his mind.

Yet Laizer still didn't express his feelings or allow his expression to reveal them. Instead, he only said, "Have a safe trip home," as he would with any other client.

"I'll miss you," Kim responded.

When Laizer said nothing in return, Kim simply gave him her email address and phone number and asked him to stay in touch. Then she flashed him her brilliant smile and turned away before he could see the tears rolling down her cheeks. Laizer waved as she headed through security to board a plane and fly out of his life.

18

WHEN LAIZER RETURNED TO ARUSHA, HIS friends, who knew he had fallen for Kim, plied him with questions.

"What happened with Kim?" one asked.

"Well, she left," Laizer replied, expressionless.

"You wasted all your time and now she is gone to the other side of the world," another said, shaking his head. "You know you will never see her again. Ever."

"I know," Laizer responded. But then he reached into his pocket and felt that little piece of paper with Kim's email on it.

Once Laizer returned home to Naiyobi, he would be far from electricity, cell phones, or internet, but while he was in Arusha, he could send emails. Before leaving Arusha, he stopped at an internet café and tentatively started typing:

```
Hi Kim.
How are you doing? Did you get home
safely? How is your family?
```

Laizer hit send and sat back to take a few deep breaths. Then, before he even had a chance to turn off the computer, he received an email back.

```
Hi Laizer.
I got home safely. Thanks so much for
going with me to Kilimanjaro and guiding
me in your Maasai culture. I really
appreciated it.
```

It was that easy. Laizer and Kim began corresponding regularly—at least, when Laizer was in town and could get on a computer—and occasionally even spoke on the phone. This went on for the next eight months.

In their emails, they discussed the great opportunity the Baxter Award had provided to Kim. She asked Laizer what he would do with a Baxter Award. He responded that he would use the resources to obtain a mountain-guiding license because with it he would earn enough money to attend college and have more opportunities. Wanting to "pay it forward," Kim decided to sponsor Laizer to do just that. Laizer took a course to obtain his mountain-guiding license, all the while keeping her updated. During those months, Laizer emailed or called Kim while he was in Arusha, but when the course was over, they communicated less because he spent much more time back in Naiyobi.

And life in Naiyobi was hard. In fact, it was harder than ever before, so Laizer was plenty distracted. He had grown up in Naiyobi without cultivated food, but after the NCAA began to allow some cultivation in 1992, families had learned to depend upon the corn and potatoes they grew to keep from starving. But then the NCAA found that the Maasai population was increasing exponentially; rather than topping out at twenty thousand, as had been expected, the population was almost one hundred thousand. The NCAA feared that at this rate of increase, it wouldn't be long before the Maasai's cattle would irreparably harm the forage needed for the NCA's famous wildlife.

In 2007, to reduce the numbers of Maasai living in the NCA, the NCAA once again started to forbid cultivation, with enforcement beginning in 2009, in the hopes that it would encourage the Maasai to leave the area. The NCAA also mandated that anyone who had arrived after 1959 had six months to relocate to somewhere outside the park. In all, somewhere between two thousand and five thousand Naiyobi residents were uprooted—most of them uneducated and unprepared to find any other type of work once they relocated.

The exodus included Laizer's maternal grandmother and grandfather. Laizer remembers his mother crying as her parents left town and headed north to Loliondo. Laizer's friend Yohana, who was working in Karatu, moved his family to Loliondo too. Those who stayed started buying their crops from the outside—if they could. Finding the resources to purchase food was almost impossible for these poor families. The NCAA planned to bring in food to the remaining Maasai people, but deliveries were unpredictable. During the rains, when the road washed away, the NCAA drivers couldn't get to Naiyobi, and during the dry spells, they never brought enough.

Laizer's trips to town became critical for resupplying his family with bags of rice. The trips also provided Laizer with his own critical dose of time with Kim through email or calls. When speaking of home, Laizer mostly kept it light, acknowledging the challenges of the Maasai without revealing the true depths of their suffering. He was also careful never to reveal his feelings, an easy undertaking for a man trained as a Maasai warrior. But in December, Laizer received an

115

email from Kim that got to the point of what they'd both been avoiding.

She wrote:

```
Sometimes it seems you are writing to a
friend and sometimes it seems you have
deeper feelings. I feel like we can stay
on the path we've been on, which is
comfortable and safe, or go down a new
and exciting one, uncertain of what lies
ahead. But I don't want to misinterpret
your messages and go down the wrong one.
The direction I choose depends on your
feelings. Can you help me understand what
you are feeling?
```

Laizer replied the next day with a short email saying only that he would be in touch soon. Then he shut down the computer and went to consult with a group of friends, most of whom were confused about his attraction to a white woman.

"Why would you want to pursue a blood woman?" one of them wondered aloud.

"She's a donkey," said another.

But Yohana, his best friend, who had spent more time around foreigners and was more open to supporting his friend's interest, didn't shun the idea. Instead, he gave some advice.

"Try writing her back. You never know what she'll say. Just don't worry."

But Laizer did worry. For while he didn't have the words for it, he knew that his friends' reaction—calling a white woman "blood woman" or "donkey"—was the reaction he would also get from his family. Worse, he had heard of the prejudices that existed against black men and, as a safari guide, was well aware of the power differential safari tourists held over him. Since Kim was a white woman, any accusations of inappropriate behavior by her could get him fired. Laizer also knew that, realistically, he would never see her again, as was true of all the other safari clients. But even as Laizer's friends teased him, he couldn't stop talking about Kim.

Finally, Yohana, who was fairly pragmatic, said, "I think she just wants to know how you feel."

"What if she becomes angry? I could get fired," Laizer responded.

"Come on. If that is the worst that happens, you can find another job."

Finally, after three days of delaying, Laizer wrote Kim back. He told her everything. He told her that he had loved her from the beginning. He told her that he loved her quiet, considerate kindness. He told her that he had volunteered to go to Mt. Kilimanjaro just to be with her. He told her that he had stayed in Arusha an extra week just to see her one last time. With the time difference, Laizer didn't know when Kim would read his words, so he pushed send and tried to distract himself by browsing the news on the internet. Within a half hour, there was a reply.

With his heart thumping, he clicked on it.

```
Laizer,
I was waiting all this time for you to
say this. What took you so long? I don't
want to live in Tanzania, but would you
```

```
like to visit the United States and see
what life is really like here and if you
would like it?
```

For, unbeknownst to Laizer, Kim had also been confiding in friends and family and seeking advice. While most didn't seem to know what to say to a friend who'd fallen in love with a Maasai warrior, Kim's brother's comment of, "What do you have to lose, Kim? The cost of a plane ticket?" gave her the confidence to take a chance.

19

THUS BEGAN LAIZER'S PREPARATIONS FOR TRAVEL to the U.S., which, for a person growing up in a remote, traditional Maasai village in northern Tanzania, is something of an ordeal. He didn't just need a passport and visa. He first needed a birth certificate to get a passport. To obtain a birth certificate, he needed his parents' help. This meant telling his very traditional parents about his white girlfriend from the other side of the world. Since the Maasai have no equivalent to dating and engagement, Laizer decided to keep it simple and just tell them he'd found the person he wanted to marry, and that in order to marry her he needed to travel to the United States.

"What, you can't find anyone to marry in all of Tanzania or even Kenya?" Mekuru fumed.

"It isn't about finding someone to marry. It is about finding someone I love," Laizer said. "There are many tribes who marry for love."

"Love? What is love anyway?" Mekuru raged.

"You know love," Laizer explained. "You know love because you love your children."

"Marriage is not about love," Mekuru responded.

"Many tribes marry for love. I want to marry for love," Laizer said.

"You tried that," his father spat. "You chased Gracie like a fool and it failed. You failed."

"I will not fail with Kim," Laizer replied, his heart pounding. "And I need your support to make it happen."

Mekuru walked away but, in time, agreed to help Laizer if it meant his firstborn son would finally marry and have children. Laizer quickly began arrangements.

The first step was obtaining a birth certificate. Having been born in a dark enkaji in a remote village, within a tribe that recognized age sets instead of individuals, Laizer had no idea about his birth year, let alone his birth date. His mother, however, remembered that during the fall of the year he was born, there were planes continually flying over Naiyobi, preparing for war with Uganda.

With this information, Laizer figured out that he was born in 1978. Naalamala also remembered the weather that day, from which Laizer could guess an approximate birth month. With this information, he walked the sixty or so miles to the NCAA district headquarters in Loliondo to obtain a birth certificate, and then to the local court for the judge's approval.

With birth certificate in hand, Laizer then caught a bus to Arusha to finally procure his passport. When the state department issued him a passport with the wrong birth year—1984 instead of 1978—he overlooked it because he was so pleased to have finally received the passport. But when he told Kim, she explained, "You need to get it changed. It needs to be right. This is an official document." When he went to get it corrected, the state department office said his parents would have to go in person to Dar es Salaam, the largest city in Tanzania, to fix it. So Laizer traveled by both daladala and foot back to Naiyobi and asked his parents to make the journey. When they agreed, he gave them a cow as a thank-you gift.

Together, Laizer and his parents walked twenty-five miles to Engaruka, took a daladala to Arusha, and then took a city bus for ten hours to Dar es Salaam. Naalamala had never been outside Naiyobi, and Mekuru had never been past Karatu. Neither had ever been in a daladala or bus. The traffic was so bad in Dar that Laizer's parents couldn't even figure out how to cross the street. Laizer would hold Naalamala's hand and lead her across the road, then zigzag back for Mekuru. While in Dar, Laizer's parents were mostly quiet, stopping often to look around, and Laizer often had to nudge them to move on.

In the city, they stayed in a hotel paid for by Kim. Laizer's parents had never been inside a non-Maasai building, nor had they seen electricity, beds, or indoor bathrooms. Laizer taught Mekuru to use the bathroom, and then Mekuru taught Naalamala. Laizer knew Naalamala was overwhelmed because she barely spoke or uttered her trademark chuckle during the journey. It was only later that Laizer found out Naalamala had enjoyed that part of the trip when he overheard her telling her friends that she really liked the bed, the running water, and the cement floors.

The next day, they made it to the Tanzanian immigration office to correct his passport and obtain a visa.

While Laizer negotiated the system, he also kept working as a safari guide and stayed in touch with Kim. Talking to Kim was easy, even with the lingering language barrier. Sometimes their conversations would focus on Kim's life in the United States. Other times, Laizer would tell stories about what happened on his safaris. Sometimes Laizer even called Kim while on safari and told her about the wildlife they were seeing. One particularly memorable phone conversation happened at a safari camp, when Laizer woke before sunrise to use the bathroom.

On that particular morning, when Laizer had tried to push open the bathroom door, it felt like it was locked. As he waited, he heard a *grrrrr* and figured maybe a hyena was trapped inside. He pushed the door hard to encourage the animal to run out, but when he did, he heard the sound again and realized it was a lion. When he yelled, "Lion in the bathroom!" people came running until there were about two hundred gathered around at this public campground.

Laizer radioed the ranger, who arrived planning to kill the lion. But Laizer said, "You can't kill it with all these people here taking pictures." Instead, they called the closest veterinarian, who was three hours away in Karatu. While they waited, Laizer attempted to get his safari group to go on a game drive and observe other lions, but none of them budged—they were all fascinated by the lion in the bathroom. So Laizer found himself with some free time and called Kim. He described the whole ordeal to her as he waited for the veterinarian to arrive, and they laughed about how Laizer was now being referred to as "the lucky guy who almost died in the bathroom."

Finally, many months, calls, and safari trips later, Laizer had his birth certificate, passport with the correct date of birth, and visa. He was ready. His family must have been in denial up to this point, because when he announced he was leaving for the United States, they tried to talk him out of it. It wasn't that marrying outside of one's tribe was new in Tanzania or even forbidden among the Maasai; it was that Kim was lived so far away.

His mother cried to him that she was afraid he would never come back. Laizer's flying in an airplane would be another first and was therefore completely unfamiliar to the residents of Naiyobi. Although everyone in the village had seen airplanes fly overhead, they had never seen one up close. They had only seen a helicopter up close once, when a group had come to photograph an eruption of the Ol Doinyo Lengai volcano.

It was also a problem for Laizer's family that Kim was white. Laizer's father and one of his uncles tried to make Laizer understand that because Kim was white, she was not fully a woman. They even called Laizer into a special meeting to try and convince him that he was simply following a "donkey" who wasn't worth his time. No one in his family could believe that he couldn't find someone to marry in all of Tanzania. Only Loserian, the brother who had taken on Laizer's arranged marriage for him, was supportive. He said, "Go and marry her if it is what you want." And it was what Laizer wanted.

Laizer told Kim he was ready to come visit, and she bought him a plane ticket to the United States. Before Laizer left, Naalamala presented Laizer with a hand-beaded wedding dress for Kim. Naalamala, along with the rest of the family, assumed he was going to the United States to marry Kim.

20

WHEN LAIZER ARRIVED AT THE SAN Francisco airport in April of 2009, he was held up at customs for no reason he could discern. Once cleared, he rushed to follow the last of the crowd to the baggage claim. From a sea of luggage, Laizer picked up his one small bag and headed for the exit. His exhaustion from traveling for two days straight, in ways that were completely foreign to him, was overcome by his exhilaration and nervousness about finally being with Kim. There she was—her face lit up with the brilliant smile he had longed to see. Kim walked right up to Laizer and gave him a warm, welcoming hug. They laughed at the awkwardness in their language as she led him to her car.

Kim asked Laizer if there was anything he particularly wanted to see on their way to her family's house. He didn't know. He hadn't thought much about seeing anything upon his arrival—other than her. So they decided to head straight to her parents' house. On the drive, Laizer was amazed by the highways and buildings and wondered how they could even have been constructed. They talked about Laizer's trip in the airplane, and Kim briefed him on her parents: her mother was very talkative while her father was quiet.

When they pulled up to the house, Kim's parents came outside to greet them and usher them inside. Laizer had brought clothes for colder temperatures, so they loaned him T-shirts, which were more suitable for the hot weather. Then they all did their best to have a group conversation, with Kim's parents speaking slowly and Laizer working hard at enunciating his stilted English. Kim and Laizer stayed for just a few hours with her parents before heading to Kim's house in Foresta, a tiny village of fewer than fifty homes surrounded by Yosemite National Park. In just a two-and-a-half-hour drive, they traveled from the heat of the crowded Central Valley to cooler temperatures in this little village in the mountains.

When they arrived, Laizer pulled the hand-beaded dress his mother had made from his bag and presented it to Kim. Just as Laizer couldn't explain to his mother exactly why he was traveling to the United States to see a woman he was in love with but wasn't sure he was going to marry, he couldn't tell Kim that he was presenting her with a marriage dress. Instead, he described it as a thank-you gift for paying for his guiding class. He allowed himself that one little lie to bridge the cultural gap, even though he always suspected she knew the truth.

Kim worked during the first month of Laizer's two-month visit. Since Kim worked in Yosemite Valley and Laizer hadn't seen it yet, he decided to accompany her to the valley and explore the area while she worked. He wore his Maasai garb and found a large walking stick to carry. He then walked up to the top of Yosemite Falls. When he got back to the bottom, a woman walked right up to him.

"Are you Laizer?" she asked confidently.

"Yes. How did you know?" he responded.

"Not many people show up in Yosemite in a Maasai outfit with a huge walking stick!" she laughed. "I'm Catherine, a close friend of Kim's."

"Oh. Kim." Laizer flashed a smile.

After they chatted, Laizer continued his explorations by walking to Mirror Lake and then to the top of Nevada Fall. In that one day, he did all the major hikes in the valley. At the end of the workday, when he told Kim where he'd been, at first she didn't believe him. But he had the photos to prove it. Although he'd grown up in one of the most stunning landscapes on earth, his first views of Yosemite Valley astounded him.

Laizer tried to settle into being on his own for the rest of the month, but it was challenging. Not only was he away from his large family, but most of the people who lived in Foresta were working or visiting the park during the day. Instead of being surrounded by family and community, as he had been in Naiyobi, he was completely alone. The village of Foresta, which was less remote than Naiyobi in terms of its proximity to a store and civilization, was a world away from life in Naiyobi, where days were spent tending cattle to assure there was at least something to put in their bellies. At night, though, he felt a connection between the two villages, which were both surrounded by endless stars and quiet.

How could such a stunning place with access to natural food and clean water be so empty of people? Laizer was surprised to learn there had once been many more people living in Foresta and throughout Yosemite. He found evidence of former tribal occupancy after he learned to spot rocky outcroppings where acorns had been pounded into flour, and to recognize forests that had been modified by intentional burning. Like Naiyobi, all evidence of tribal existence was organic. Laizer contemplated how it must have been much more peaceful long ago because now, even though Foresta was small and vacant, the nearby Yosemite Valley was often packed with cars and the noise, trash, and smog that came with them. Where had those earlier residents gone and why? Is this what would happen in Ngorongoro if the Maasai were forced to leave, to be replaced with an increase in tourism and all its trappings?

To occupy his days, Laizer often drove into the valley with Kim to hike while she worked. Sometimes he hiked the twelve miles from Kim's home to the valley just to visit her at work. On other days, he would take long walks and explore the beautiful land on his own. In just a few days, Laizer had hiked all the main trails he could access in Yosemite, and he ended up doing most trails multiple times. The scenery was beautiful, but he missed the wide-open vistas and bountiful wildlife of the Serengeti Plains. When he was at Kim's all alone, he struggled with loneliness and tried to distract himself by learning to cook, doing laundry, and taking walks. But the days dragged.

At night and on the weekends, Laizer's boredom wasn't an issue because Kim was around. Plus, she introduced him to her friends. Together, they taught Laizer new sports like kayaking and biking. While it was great to meet people, the more people he met, the more awkward and limited he found his English. In Tanzania, when people spoke English, they spoke it slowly, so Laizer thought he knew it. But when he got to California, he couldn't follow the conversation because everyone spoke very quickly and used slang.

Along with the language barrier, Laizer was often uncomfortable with the weather. In Tanzania, there was a much smaller range of temperatures. In Yosemite in April, Laizer was in snow some of the time and in extreme heat at other times. He also struggled with stomach trouble from food he wasn't used to eating; despite his turning to rice for solace, his stomach issues lasted the entire trip.

Kim took the second month of Laizer's visit off to travel with him. Laizer was so ready to focus on her that he immediately asked her to marry him, but she said, "Oh, no, we need to know each other much better first." He didn't understand why they needed to wait, but being true to his Maasai upbringing, he kept quiet about it.

Laizer was so quiet that Kim couldn't understand why he seemed so down when they were heading off on what she thought was a dream trip. The plan was to start by visiting Kings Canyon and Sequoia National Parks and then drive up to Lake Tahoe. Even as they were packing the car, Kim knew something was wrong. She tried to get him to engage with her about his feelings, but he just wouldn't communicate to her the anxiety he felt about their relationship or his opinions about what they were doing.

Finally, while there were backpacking in Kings Canyon, Laizer's veneer cracked.

"Why are we doing this?" he asked.

"Doing what? Backpacking?" Kim responded.

"Yes, backpacking. Why are we doing this?"

"I thought you loved backpacking," Kim stopped to look at Laizer, her expression betraying her disappointment.

"No. I backpack on Kilimanjaro because it is my job. I lead the clients, and the porters carry everything. I never wanted to be a porter. This is more like punishment," Laizer said harshly.

"Are you kidding me?" Kim asked through tears.

"No, I would never do that," Laizer replied, softening. He thought she had said, "Are you *killing* me?" but he didn't elaborate on why he would never do that, so Kim didn't have a chance to clarify.

"What do you want to do?" Kim prodded, taking a deep breath and waiting for Laizer to reply. "Please. Talk to me."

"Let's just hike," Laizer replied, avoiding the request for a more intimate conversation.

At the end of the two months, Laizer was ready to leave. He regretted giving up his job and wasting two months of his life chasing a woman who didn't want to marry him. It wasn't because he was older than other Maasai men when they marry, as they traditionally marry after their warriorhood has ended, but because of all the investment of time and heartache. Although Kim insisted she wanted their relationship to progress and to meet his parents, Laizer didn't believe her since they weren't engaged. When he left, Laizer assumed they were breaking up.

21

IN JUNE, WHEN LAIZER ARRIVED BACK in Tanzania, he was dejected. He spent the first night in Arusha, where he met up with Yohana.

"How did it go?" Yohana asked.

"She told me she isn't ready to marry me," Laizer answered honestly. "I need to move on." But the next morning, before Laizer left Arusha, Laizer received an email from Kim.

```
I bought a ticket to come to Tanzania
to spend time with your family and then
a month later for both of us to return
to California. If you come back and
volunteer at Yosemite, we can see what
it's really like to be together when we
are both working.
```

Laizer couldn't believe it, but he embraced the news and went back to Naiyobi with more confidence. This time he had money, so he took a daladala to the Sopa Lodge on the rim of the Ngorongoro Crater and then walked the last forty-five miles home. Laizer had been the first person from Naiyobi to fly away in an airplane, and here he was, back in the village. The attention that brought was exciting because he also had confidence that he and Kim would end up together.

Everyone wanted to know what it was like to fly in an airplane and go to America. Laizer showed pictures and described the skyscrapers, highways, elaborate homes, grocery stores with all manner of foods, restaurants, bridges, airplanes and airports, and the waterfalls of Yosemite. And Laizer told his father about the cattle. He said that it isn't true that the Maasai have all the cattle because there were cattle in California. Mekuru glanced at him and said, "Of course there are, because the white people came and took them."

A few months later, Laizer met Kim in Arusha. They stayed at Laizer's boss's house, which served as their base for the month. First, they took some trips out of Arusha, and then they traveled to Naiyobi. For their arrival in Naiyobi, Kim wore the beaded dress Laizer's mother had made for her, which, unbeknownst to her, was a bridal outfit. As such, after they arrived by Jeep in the center of town, villagers lined the paths to greet them, bless them, and walk with them the mile and a half to Laizer's family's angan'g.

Laizer's family was sweet and welcoming. With Kim only speaking basic Swahili and a few words of Maa, and Laizer's family only speaking Maa—with only a few of them speaking basic Swahili—spoken conversations were impossible. Instead, they did their best by communicating with hugs and kindness. With Kim's vibrant smile and Naalamala's amiable chuckle, the two most important women in Laizer's life managed to get along well.

One day, Laizer found a friend who could translate, so Kim could have a more substantial conversation with his parents, and his parents could ensure Laizer wasn't misinterpreting Kim's words. There was also communication through song. Kim and one of Laizer's sisters had fun just sitting together and singing the Tanzanian national anthem. Laizer and Kim visited with family during the day and retreated to the old ranger post each night, where they had their own room, since no one was staying there at the time. There, Kim also had her own food and stove to cook meals.

Laizer and Kim traveled back to Arusha for some time on their own and spent the last week in Zanzibar. Since Laizer had never been to Zanzibar, it was a treat to explore some of his country as a tourist, and even more so to have this adventure with Kim. But as they traveled, cultural differences revealed some cracks in their relationship.

The first big one occurred when they went on a long hike one morning without eating anything beforehand. After going steadily for five hours, Laizer turned around and saw Kim's eyes starting to tear up. Alarmed, he asked what was wrong. "I'm out of energy," she said quietly. "My blood sugar is low." Laizer didn't understand what that meant because, despite his living in a feast-to-famine cycle for much of his life, he had never felt that way. *How could she be so affected by food when she gets to eat every day? Even multiple times a day?* he wondered. *How often have my sisters gone without food and never said a word?*

He asked Kim why she hadn't spoken up before so they could have turned around. When she answered that it was because she wanted to reach the summit, he became further confused. Maybe she wasn't weak but just open with her emotions in a way Maasai women were never permitted.

The treatment of women certainly affected Laizer's sisters and mothers, but it also affected Kim. For Kim, the sexism caused her to bristle physically. In Maasai culture, when you greet someone on the road, the men all shake hands and introduce the women last. When Kim would finally be introduced, the men would acknowledge her for just a moment and then quickly resume their own conversation—sometimes even turning their backs to her.

After spending time in college, cities, and in the United States, as well as witnessing how men in his village interacted with the woman he loved, Laizer began to think more and more about the Maasai men's traditional treatment of women. Laizer became introspective. He realized how his Maasai sisters never had enough food or any other trappings of an easy or equitable life, and how they were never allowed to speak out against it.

Language was also a challenge. Navigating languages that were so different from each of their native tongues was draining and left little room for being "close enough." Kim could barely speak Swahili, let alone Maa. Laizer could communicate in English, but only if conversations were slow, simple, and precise. For both Kim and Laizer, the effort was exhilarating—and exhausting. It was also the cause of many misunderstandings.

There were also smaller issues that added up. Laizer was used to being surrounded by family and friends, whom he missed when in American society. Kim was used to heading off on her own to run or bike, and she couldn't do that safely in either the Serengeti Plains or Tanzanian cities. Much like how Laizer felt unsafe in American cities, Kim felt unsafe in some of the Tanzanian cities.

When Laizer and Kim attempted to figure out how a relationship could work between them, they had all these issues to consider. But Kim was clear on one thing—she could either live in the United States full time, or half time in each country, but not full time in Tanzania. Thinking about being separated from her family and country for long periods overwhelmed her and made her tear up. Laizer agreed that they could live in the United States, but he wouldn't discuss it in more detail. Unbeknownst to either of them, their communication issues came from the cultures where they had grown up.

In Maasai culture, crying was reserved for only the strongest of emotions, and looking at someone in the eye was reserved for anger. In American culture, crying is a common way of expressing emotion, and eye contact is expected. On Kim's end, she couldn't understand why Laizer didn't look her in the eye when they were having deep conversations. Did he not respect her? And why was it so difficult for him to communicate his feelings? On Laizer's end, he couldn't understand why Kim would cry with emotion. But they were both determined to navigate these cultural differences because of their love for each other. At the end of the month, they flew back to the United States to see where it would take their relationship.

22

FLYING INTO SAN FRANCISCO THAT DECEMBER with Kim at his side was an entirely different experience for Laizer. During this trip, Laizer was traveling to a known destination, had a volunteer position waiting for him, and was confident in his relationship. This visit would be a bit longer—four months—and Laizer intended to get engaged before he returned home. It was also much different to arrive in December, when the tiny village of Foresta was covered in snow. Before starting work, Laizer's first order of business was to find a way to stay warm, which ended up being by wearing double layers of pants.

Laizer's volunteer position was in the Yosemite National Park Visitor Center in Yosemite Valley. His boss, Erik Westerlund, had met Laizer the previous year and had full confidence Laizer would excel in the position. Erik was a longtime Yosemite ranger with distinctive curly auburn hair and a ready laugh. The job involved working behind the visitor center desk and getting people acquainted with the park. When Erik offered Laizer the job, he offer reassurance that Laizer was fully qualified.

"Yosemite is a big and complex park, but between your degrees and your time as a safari guide, you have all the credentials to do great," Erik told him.

"Okay. I can do that," Laizer assured him.

And he could. Even operating in English, which was his third language and pretty rough, Laizer confidently took on the job. Every now and then, visitors would ask him where he was from, due to his accent, and he would light up. He was happiest when he got to share his Maasai stories. He even went to the local elementary school to tell stories from home and got rave reviews.

Laizer's coworkers also loved to hear his stories. Sometimes the stories were inspired by questions.

"Since most Maasai don't have access to glasses, does bad eyesight select out of the population?" Erik asked one day.

"Unfortunately, there is a lot of late-life blindness due to disease," Laizer would explain.

"What about teeth?" another ranger named Andy Steele asked. "You have such nice teeth. Is that because of all the milk you drank as a kid?"

"Probably," Laizer responded. "But we do brush our teeth. We just use a peeled stick instead of a plastic toothbrush."

"What about water?" Andy continued. "The rest of us are all sitting here sweating and drinking all day and you don't even have a water bottle. How is that possible?"

"We don't have access to water when we go on long walks, so I am being careful not to get used to drinking it," Laizer answered. "Although I do make exceptions." He grinned widely as he flashed a hidden can of Orange Crush, for which he had developed a weakness.

Many of the rangers Laizer worked with became friends with whom he could get together during his time off, especially because he and Kim rarely had the same two days off. Andy and others taught Laizer to ski and snowshoe, which was fun and allowed for more introspection. One time, while Laizer was skiing with a friend named Winston, Laizer asked Winston who had taught him to ski.

"My parents taught me to ski when I was three," Winston answered.

"Three? In Naiyobi, we didn't have time for fun like that at age three; we were learning to keep the calves and lambs safe," Laizer observed.

Once spring came, skiing turned to hiking. Another coworker, Paul Ollig, asked Laizer to take him on a real "Maasai hike." They started at one a.m. to go up the Four Mile Trail. Then they walked over to the top of Half Dome, then Cloud's Rest, and up to Upper Yosemite Fall. But when they got to the top of Cloud's Rest, Paul was done, so they hiked back to the car. Little did Paul know that Laizer would do it all again the next week with Andy Esparza, but after Cloud's Rest, they would continue all the way to Tenaya Lake, take a few side trails, continue to Yosemite Falls, and then walk back, for a total of around forty miles.

Paul, however, was game for more. When Laizer said he needed a day-hiking buddy for when Kim backpacked or kayaked with her friends, Paul was ready. Laizer and Paul hiked all over that summer, with every hike being twenty miles or more. But even as Paul got in shape, he continued to be amazed at Laizer's ability hike without stopping. Once, after hiking eighteen miles, Paul stopped to chug water as Laizer sipped a Mountain Dew and commented, "I wish I was in better shape. I bet I can't even run fifty kilometers without water anymore."

Another time, Laizer and Paul were hiking back in the dark and talking about their relationships with women during their teenage years.

"Maasai teens and young men think that spending time with women weakens them, so they avoid contact with women to be strong and fast," Laizer explained to Paul. "When you run in a group of Maasai men and fall behind, the others hit you with a stick and tease you, saying, 'You must have kissed a woman who stole your magic.'"

Jeez, I would have been a really fast Maasai," Paul joked.

Laizer loved those hikes with Paul, and vice versa. They spent their time together joking and telling stories, which inspired a lot of self-reflection.

In addition to Andy, Erik, and Paul, Laizer made several other close friends that spring, each of them remembering him as stoic and serious at first, in keeping with his Maasai upbringing, and then openhearted with a wide smile. One night, a friend of Kim's threw a dinner party, so more of their friends could meet Laizer.

That was the night Laizer met Dave and Jill Engelstad, who were about to go on safari in northern Tanzania. Dave was thoughtful and generous, and Jill was a powerhouse of creativity. Laizer offered to look over their itinerary and give them helpful ideas and information. They soon became good friends who would discuss all kinds of cultural differences and ideas for bridging these gaps. These friendships were good for Laizer, but they were also good for Laizer and Kim's relationship, as each new friend would knock away another bit of the armor that kept Laizer from sharing his feelings—particularly with Kim.

Socially, this second visit to the United States stood in stark contrast to the first. Laizer was busy, had meaningful volunteer work, and made many friends. Laizer was better at adjusting to California's extreme temperatures and digesting its food. Laizer and Kim had also worked through some of the awkwardness they'd faced last time. From Laizer's perspective, Kim wasn't tearing up as much, and even when she did, such as during a movie, Laizer was less disturbed by it. And Laizer was starting to open up more and more to Kim. But Laizer was still focused on marriage. Waiting for Kim to welcome his proposal became increasingly difficult as the weeks passed. He was ready to commit, but was she?

Finally, with three weeks left of the visit, Kim invited Laizer on a skiing trip to Yosemite's Clark Range Overlook. She brought a blanket and sparkling apple cider and gave him a card to read. In it, she had written her reflections about what she would need in order to marry Laizer, and what she suspected he needed to marry her. She wrote, "If we can both agree to these things, I'm ready to commit to spending my life with you." Laizer read the letter and broke into a big grin.

Together, they examined the list. It included Kim's need to have her home base in the United States and, when they were in Tanzania, to be stationed in a place where she could be free to move about without fear for her safety. Laizer's needs included saving to buy a house and eventually having or adopting children. None of the items on the list were insurmountable. Laizer's heart was thumping as he placed a ring on Kim's finger.

Laizer had been waiting for this moment for so long, and it was finally happening with the woman he loved in this beautiful place. While Laizer didn't know what engagement meant exactly, he knew it led to marriage.

Then it was time to travel back to Tanzania to begin the process of obtaining a fiancé visa, so Laizer could remain in the United States. Laizer and Kim expected it to take about a month. Little did they know the difficulties Laizer would face.

23

As it turned out, getting a fiancé visa was a much more complex process than getting a tourist visa. To make things worse, Laizer's passport and birth certificate were stolen in Arusha. He filed a police report, and, miraculously, his documents were found and returned to him about a week later. Laizer then returned to Dar to begin a rigorous process of immunization, including testing for tuberculosis, HIV, and malaria. The many immunizations required multiple trips to Dar because some could not be done within the same week. The process was also expensive, requiring Laizer to sell five cows to pay for it all.

Between trips, Laizer normally stayed in Arusha with friends, but during longer layovers he traveled to Naiyobi. There, he would adopt the Maasai lifestyle but entertain family and friends with images of life in California. Notably, he recounted stories of snow and skiing to his mother, but she didn't believe it was true until he showed her the videos on his phone.

Laizer enjoyed this time with family and friends, but it was painful to wait for the visa, never knowing when it would be ready. Also, amid the good times came tragedy. One evening, when Laizer was working in Naalamala's angan'g, a relative called out, "I can't find my kid! I can't find my kid!" Laizer asked the other children if they knew where the lost one was. They replied that they'd heard him crying while he'd wandered "that way," and they pointed west. Following a trail of blood and pieces of clothing, Laizer and the other adults eventually came upon the three-year-old's head hanging in a tree. It was the work of a leopard. One man climbed up and brought down the child's remains. As is customary of Maasai, the child was never spoken of again. Even so, the sorrow of this devastation lay thick over the village, and it made Laizer long for Kim.

Yet the process of getting a visa was so slow that Laizer began to doubt what he was doing. At one point, the NCAA offered him a job working within the NCA, and he almost took it—but then finally, in July, after four months of working through the requirements, Laizer was issued a visa and was on his way back to the United States.

Once a fiancé visa is issued, the recipient has ninety days to get married. After marriage, one can obtain a Green Card and later apply for citizenship. In mid-September, the day after Laizer arrived in the United States, he and Kim went to the courthouse in Mariposa, a little town west of Yosemite, and were married. But they didn't even tell their own families about it, as this ceremony was just to satisfy the courts. The real wedding would be a month later with family and friends in their little village of Foresta.

Laizer had no idea what an American wedding entailed, so he consulted some of his new American friends.

"Aside from helping Kim get ready, am I supposed to prepare anything special for her?"

"All you need to remember is that no matter what she says, just say, 'I love you' back," Moose said with a sly smile. While Moose was well known for his sarcastic sense of humor, sarcasm didn't translate well, and Laizer only picked up on the part about not preparing anything.

The day before the ceremony, Kim's family arrived, and Laizer helped them cook in preparation for the guests. Laizer, still new to cooking, pitched in awkwardly. This was a much different situation from the weddings in Tanzania, where the bride and groom's friends cook and prepare. Kim's dad and sister did the bulk of the cooking, but it was a laborious task.

On the day of the wedding, as Laizer busied himself with helping, more and more people kept arriving in their small mountain town. Grateful their dearest friends and Kim's family would be there, Laizer was also heartbroken that none of his family would attend. Getting passports and traveling to the United States would never be an option for his parents because of culture, money, and politics.

Laizer thought about what this wedding would have been like had they planned a Maasai wedding in Naiyobi. It would have been a massive event, with hundreds of villagers in attendance. The villagers would have prepared food for the feast while Laizer and Kim each made lengthy family visits filled with discussions of the obligations of marriage. Once the marriage was blessed and solidified by both sets of parents, they would have joined a two-day celebration culminating in Laizer taking Kim to live in his mother's angan'g.

For a moment, it was Laizer's turn to have an emotional cry, but it was brief because the day was full of love and excitement. At one point, Kim asked Laizer if he had prepared his vows. Feeling confident that she was referring to his role of responding "I love you" to whatever she said, he confidently answered, "Yes."

Then the day of the wedding arrived, and their friends gathered at their home. Laizer's friend Winston inquired, "What did you prepare for your vows?"

Laizer answered, "I will tell her I love her."

Winston was incredulous. "That's it?"

Laizer told Winston he had checked with Moose ahead of time and learned he only needed to affirm his love. Moose, standing with them, opened his eyes wide and explained, "I was kidding." There was no time for Laizer to prepare vows, so Winston instructed Laizer not to worry; he should just express why he loves her, why he wants to marry her, and how he will be committed to her. Laizer felt a wave of panic, and then it was time for the ceremony.

The wedding was outside, overlooking a meadow. Andy was Laizer's best man; Molly, a friend Kim had met at Yosemite, was Kim's maid of honor; and Erik Westerlund officiated. During the ceremony, Catherine, the friend who had remarked on Laizer's walking stick at Yosemite, stood up to share the couple's story, including using little American and Tanzanian flags and a small model airplane as visuals. During her vows, Kim spoke eloquently, relaying how Laizer made her want to be a better person.

And then it was Laizer's turn. He had no vows prepared but simply spoke straight from his heart.

"I really love you, Kim," Laizer started. "You have my heart and you are my family."

As he continued, Kim teared up, as did several of those in attendance.

Afterward, they partied and danced, and Laizer performed the high jumps called "adumus" that warriors do at all celebrations. During his toast, Kim's dad said, "I'm just glad Kim finally found someone who can walk as far as she can."

At one point during the festivities, Laizer couldn't find Kim. When he asked a friend, "Have you seen my wife?" he recognized that after all these months, his marriage to Kim was finally real.

Then it was time for the honeymoon. Laizer's friends told him a honeymoon was a time for the couple to relax after all the work of the wedding. There are no honeymoons in Maasai culture, but then again, there is no work for the couple to do in preparation for a Masaii wedding, either. Laizer, who was emotionally exhausted from the wedding, looked forward to relaxing. They drove to Sedona, Arizona, to spend a week at a friend's timeshare, where they could unwind and visit the Grand Canyon. After having grown up in the Serengeti, there were few views that impressed Laizer, but just as his first view of Yosemite stunned him, so did his first view of the Grand Canyon.

After the honeymoon, while Laizer was looking for a job, he did some landscaping for Kim's dad. In exchange for Laizer's labor, his father-in-law gave the younger man his old television set. While watching it, Laizer stumbled upon the show *The Bachelor*. When he told Kim about it and asked if what he'd seen was how he should have proposed, she laughed until there were tears in her eyes.

Thus began the couple's married life in the United States. Their first year, it turned out, was much harder than they'd anticipated.

24

Now that Laizer and Kim were to be together forever, Laizer wanted to focus on his goal of buying a house. To do that, he would need to find employment. Within a month, Laizer obtained his work permit, a separate document from the Green Card he would obtain later. It made sense, with a degree in wildlife management, that Laizer would find a job working for Yosemite's Research & Wildlife Management program. The problem was that in order to work for the National Park Service, Laizer would have to be a United States citizen. Tanzania does not allow for dual citizenship, and Laizer couldn't give up his Tanzanian citizenship to become an American citizen, as that would mean he would have to start paying one hundred dollars per day to visit his family since they lived in a government-run park.

Since Laizer couldn't work for the national park, it made sense for him to work as a veterinarian because of his degree in veterinary science. But to do that, Laizer would have to work in a larger town, the closest of which was two and a half hours away. Not only would Laizer have to rent his own apartment and live away from Kim during the week, but he would also have to spend time and money becoming certified to work in the United States. So becoming a veterinarian wasn't a viable option either.

Laizer tried to be creative in his job search, but the months rolled past and he still could not find a job. To avoid being alone in Foresta, he once again volunteered in the visitor center, but he was increasingly frustrated at being unable to find paid work. He tried to pick up additional skills by obtaining certification as a Wilderness First Responder. The teaching was difficult for Laizer to understand because it was in English, yet the skills seemed simple to him because of all his years living out in the Serengeti Plains.

Laizer's struggle with employment was emblematic of what many immigrants face: their skills, regardless of how proficient, are neither valued nor translatable to their new country. Without employment, Laizer did not feel fulfilled or productive, and he wasn't able to contribute financially to his marriage. Additionally, he was homesick for Naiyobi and his family, but he couldn't leave the United States to visit home until he obtained his Green Card, which would take an entire year.

Although there was the added challenge of the remoteness of each of their families' homes—in Foresta and Naiyobi—technological advances provided Laizer with some relief from his homesickness. While Laizer was using his cell phone to communicate with Julius, who was living in Arusha, they brainstormed how Laizer could call his family each week. Together, they came up with a plan that overcame the lack of electricity in Naiyobi and ensured that the timing of calls would allow Laizer's family to walk to cell reception in daylight to be safe from wildlife. To implement the plan,

Julius got a cell phone for Laizer's family. To keep the phone working, Laizer's family would charge it at the ranger station, which was the only place in all of Naiyobi that had electricity, which was generated by a solar panel.

Then on Saturday mornings, once the sun was up and they would be safer from wild animals, two or more members of Laizer's family would walk two hours to a place that had cell reception. Once there, they would call Laizer using Google Voice. Laizer, receiving the calls on Friday night in California, would then call them back using internet phone service to get a clearer line. After the call, Laizer's family would walk the two hours home. Although it often took several tries because the calls sometimes would randomly drop off, the plan worked, and a weekly ritual began.

Every Friday night, Laizer would sit in his front yard or living room while his family sat on a rock on a hill, and they would discuss the latest family news and politics. He would usually converse with his mother and a few of his siblings, but sometimes he would talk to his father. His family usually described situations that directly affected them. Frequently, they asked him to send money. These calls were a critical lifeline, but they were also emotionally exhausting for Laizer. While there was wilderness at both ends of the line, they were worlds apart. Laizer would hang up and look up at the same moon he knew shone over Naiyobi, feeling both connected and lonely at the same time.

Occasionally, weeks would go by without a call, and Laizer would know something was wrong. It was during one of these quiet periods when the sister he knew best was killed by a buffalo. Rather than tell Laizer, his family avoided him. It was part of their culture not to speak of the dead, and they also didn't want to share bad news. When they finally told him, the discussion was brief and they quickly changed the subject.

Other times, it was almost worse when his family did reluctantly share news about hardship or death because Laizer was limited in how he could help them. In one case, he learned that another sister's husband had beaten her, which had resulted in a brain hemorrhage that caused her death. As per Maasai custom, the children remain with the father after either a divorce or the mother's death, even when there is abuse.

There was also a time when Mekuru informed Laizer that one of his brothers was to be subject to a beating as punishment for an indiscretion. Afraid the bearing could maim or kill his brother, Laizer felt helpless. If Laizer were in Naiyobi, he would have been able to intervene, but from Foresta, there was nothing he could do to stop it.

Finally, Laizer found a job working at the front desk of a hotel—at least, that's what he'd thought, but when he showed up for work, he learned they only wanted him to work in the kitchen. Luckily, the same day, he was offered a retail position in the Yosemite visitor center's bookstore, which he eagerly accepted. With his experience volunteering in the visitor center, Laizer was an easy fit, and he started right away. It started with promise, but challenges quickly mounted, affecting both his work and home environments.

First, Laizer's immediate supervisor complained that Laizer didn't know the books well enough, so Laizer started skimming through books as quickly as he could on all his free time. Also, his supervisor wouldn't give Laizer the same days off as Kim, so he had even less time with his wife. Then there was a rockslide, which blocked Foresta from the main road, requiring Laizer and Kim to walk two miles, sometimes in the snow, just to reach the road. Once on the road, they would flag down a ride. Sometimes, Laizer would continue walking the entire twelve miles each way. For a Maasai, the distance wasn't a problem, but dealing with the snow and the resulting logistics was exhausting.

Laizer decided to talk to his supervisor about the situation. He found her at the bookstore and followed her into the office to ask for help. This was where things fell apart. She accused him of using drugs because his eyes were red, and of physically threatening her because he had entered her office. Laizer, who had never used drugs or alcohol, was heartbroken by the accusation. He wanted to quit and return to Tanzania. Kim urged him to seek a resolution, but she agreed to move to Tanzania with him for some limited period of time if the situation at work couldn't be repaired.

In the end, Laizer was called into a meeting with upper management and the supervisor who had been accusatory toward him. The manager led the meeting, and the supervisor, now remorseful for her actions, offered an apology. Laizer accepted it but continued to feel discouraged. However, soon after, he was offered a full-time position at the center that included benefits. He accepted. Whether the conflict at work was due to outright racism or cultural misunderstanding, Laizer still doesn't know, but the experience was jarring and deeply painful.

Also, he continued to have communication problems at home. Sometimes, it was due to Laizer's inexperience with sharing his thoughts and feelings. Other times, it was due to their vastly different cultural backgrounds. And all of it was made more challenging because Laizer was communicating in his third language, such as when Kim tried to tell Laizer about her need for some time alone.

"I could use a little alone time," Kim remarked.

"You want to be alone?" Laizer asked, staring at Kim wide-eyed, his jaw dropping open.

"Just for a little bit. Maybe a few hours," Kim said. "I need a little quiet. I think I'll go for a bike ride. Is that okay with you?"

"But we are married," Laizer said. "You want a divorce?"

"What? I just want to be alone for a few hours. I never want a divorce. It has nothing to do with our relationship. I'm just exhausted from all the people I talk to at work," Kim gently clarified. "Don't you ever want alone time?"

"No. I want to be with you," he said. To Laizer, who had grown up surrounded by family and community, alone time felt alienating and lonely. And despite the agreement they'd made on the night of their engagement, the couple continued to have differences in what they needed to feel fulfilled.

But during that first year in the United States, Laizer also found new hobbies that distracted him and soothed his anxieties. Watching his father-in-law's television, Laizer became a major consumer of news. He also became a major consumer of shoes. Being someone who had grown up barefoot, only receiving his first set of tire shoes when he was in his last year of primary school, and whose major mode of transportation was his feet, Laizer fell in love with shoes. Laizer also fell in love with the excitement and escape provided by Magic Mountain and Universal Studios, which couldn't have been more different from Laizer's home in Naiyobi. Still, Laizer continued to miss the simplicity and kinship of his Maasai home.

25

A YEAR AND NINE MONTHS AFTER ARRIVING in the United States to marry Kim, Laizer had his Green Card and was on his way to Tanzania for a visit. The trip to Arusha took two and a half days of continuous travel. Laizer was eager to see his family, but he still had many more hours of dusty overland travel before arriving in Naiyobi. He changed into his traditional orkarasha, along with Nike sneakers and a Timex watch, and went to meet with his old friend, Julius, who by now managed a safari company. True to his generous nature, Julius offered to drive Laizer to his village.

Energized by the excitement of being together again, they left early the next morning and filled each other in on the past year and a half. Julius had been outside of Tanzania but never to the United States, and he plied Laizer with questions about his travels. Laizer obliged Julius with stories of California and asked Julius for updates on the happenings in Tanzania. Soon they were far from the noise of the city and its bright lights and watched the sun rise over the African plains.

As Julius drove in and out of small towns, Laizer surveyed his homeland. It was a place with so much depth. He considered all its layers and how his perspectives had changed over time. He also dozed for a bit, waking when they drove through the entry gates of the Ngorongoro Conservation Area. From there, they still had several more hours of travel over bumpy dirt roads to get to Naiyobi. This travel time allowed Laizer to observe the wildlife he had missed: wildebeests and zebras, jackals, impalas, groups of spotted hyenas, a pride of lions, gazelles, and even a distant view of a beautifully camouflaged, solitary serval.

Along the way, they passed several Maasai villages, but Laizer's pulse only quickened when he spotted Naiyobi. The vibrant colors of the villagers' orkarashas and beaded adornments looked stunning against the green of the rolling hills, the brown of the enkajis, and the backdrop of Ol Doinyo Lengai. Finally, he was home—back where people owned almost no possessions, left no waste on the earth, and were surrounded by community. Leaving Julius's Land Rover at the ranger station, the two friends walked the last mile and a half to Laizer's mother's angan'g. With arms wide open, Naalamala, who had gotten word of Laizer's homecoming, was eagerly awaiting her son. As they embraced, Naalamala's eyes filled with tears of gratitude.

Julius greeted Laizer's family and then quickly headed back to Arusha to comply with the law that nonresidents must vacate the conservation area before dark. Laizer took a minute to soak up his surroundings, but soon he was greeted by a group of twenty of his age mates, including three of his brothers. Laizer hadn't been home in a year and a half, and, like Naalamala, no one had truly expected him to come back. Laizer's age mates welcomed him ecstatically and began rounding up a celebratory feast.

That night, Laizer joined his age mates in an enkaji that one of their mothers had vacated for the men's use, as was custom. As the guest of honor, Laizer would be the first to partake of the feast. He cupped his hand and reached into the communal pot, feeling the familiar warmth of fresh blood. He scooped up the liquid, along with several bits of kidney and liver, and, aware of his age mates' eyes upon him, quickly gulped it down. After taking a few handfuls, Laizer sat back and watched the others dip their unwashed hands into the pot and noisily enjoy the salty mixture.

Laizer then joined the group in butchering the goats and cooking the meat over the enkaji's central fire. Aware of the hungry horde of children watching them expectantly from outside, the warriors first roasted the children's portion of the goat, the stomach and chest, and gave it to them so they would run off and leave the warriors to their feast. In addition to wanting privacy, Maasai always share meat with others, especially children, believing death will come if they don't.

The warriors then cooked the remainder of the goat. Although they ate plenty of the savory meat, they were careful to set aside all portions that were to be distributed to others later, with the bulk going to the elders. After their meal, the warriors focused on each other—learning about a place called "Yosemite," telling stories of recent lion encounters, laughing, chanting, and filling Laizer's heart with memories of his home. Even though warriors don't drink alcohol, Laizer and his age mates became intoxicated from the impassioned storytelling and the warmth of the smoky enkaji.

When the party finally wound down in the early-morning hours, Laizer's self-conscious queasiness in drinking the once-familiar blood meal had long since given way. In its place was a deep sense of contentment and gratitude for having made the journey back to loved ones. The group returned the enkaji to its owner, and Laizer made his way under a carpet of stars to his mother's enkaji to sleep.

Laizer spent the majority of his time in Tanzania in Naiyobi, taking just a few jaunts with friends to Arusha. At home, he drank milk and ate cooked meat, and in town he ate rice, ugali (the flour-and-water mixture), and other offerings. Apart from that first night, Laizer didn't drink blood, nor did he drink the traditional soup made of acacia bark and herbs that warriors normally drink with blood meals.

Since he had spent the last year and a half in the United States eating fatty and sugary American foods, Laizer was worried his body would not be able to digest the acacia medicine to which it was no longer accustomed. Luckily, the only intestinal discomfort he suffered during his visit was from the unpasteurized milk he could no longer digest. What he once had drunk as his main source of calories now made his stomach groan and twist throughout the night.

Laizer spent his days helping his family and his nights visiting with friends, and before he knew it, it was time to return to the United States and his American wife. Julius traveled all the way back to the village, picked Laizer up, and drove him to the airport. On the way, Laizer gazed out at the giraffes as they moved fluidly across the plains. He thought about how the giraffes were perfectly designed to forage on the acacia trees, and he wondered if the acacia trees minded being almost gaudily decorated with dozens of dangling weaverbird nests. The drive was uneventful, and soon Julius was driving away, leaving Laizer at the airport.

RACHEL MAZUR

It would be another two days of travel before Laizer was back in Foresta, but the trip had been worth it. The visit to Naiyobi had refueled Laizer and made him feel more grounded when he returned to Kim. This time, coming back to the United States was so much different and so much better. Laizer was married, had a job, and was welcomed into the community. He was becoming fluent in English, understood American culture, and had American friends. It was a much smoother transition.

But after three months back in Foresta, Laizer began to notice an unfamiliar feeling in his gut and a sensation of hunger that could never be satisfied. He commented to Kim, "I think I have a parasite." They sought the advice of a local doctor, who tested him and found nothing. Remarking that the issue may be in his mind, the doctor sent him home. But the intestinal discomfort continued, and after eight months, Laizer had lost roughly thirty pounds. He told Kim, "I studied animal health, and I know what I'm talking about. That doctor was wrong. I have a parasite."

Laizer and Kim went further afield and consulted a different doctor. After listening to Laizer's story, this new doctor contacted a colleague, who sent him two pills. Laizer was never clear about where the pills had come from, but it seemed they had been sent from outside the United States. When Laizer received the pills, he immediately took them and went to bed without incident. Later that night, Laizer woke up and urgently went into the bathroom, thinking he was about to have diarrhea. But what came out wasn't human waste; it was a three-foot-long tapeworm with a rather large head.

26

IN THE FALL OF 2013, LAIZER received a call informing him that his dad was very sick. Mekuru's alcohol consumption had been increasing ever since he'd begun the alcohol distribution business, and his liver and pancreas were failing. Laizer rushed money to his parents through Julius so that his father could be taken to the hospital in Arusha. Mekuru was later transferred to a better-equipped hospital farther east in Moshi, where surgeons cut out half his liver and part of his kidney. The doctors admonished him that he would die if he ever drank again and sent him home. To the astonishment of those who knew him, Mekuru completely stopped drinking.

Had Mekuru died, Laizer would have rushed home because his family could not bury Mekuru without his oldest son present. In previous times, the family would have left Mekuru out for the wildlife to devour, as Laizer had once seen during his childhood, but the NCAA had eventually banned that custom. Fortunately, Mekuru survived. While he didn't give credit to non-Maasai medicine, he did credit Laizer for his financial and logistical help. Mekuru didn't have to sell any cattle for his medical care; Laizer had paid for everything.

Grateful to Laizer for his survival, Mekuru repented to his god. The older man was sorry for how he had treated his firstborn son and lifted the curse he'd put on Laizer so many years earlier. But that didn't stop the bad news from coming.

A few weeks after Mekuru's medical emergency, Laizer's fourth brother, Supuk, and Yohana rode together on a motorcycle to visit Laizer's father, and they crashed. Supuk was thrown through the air to the other side of the road. His leg was broken in three places, and the bone broke through his skin. It was an open fracture, but he survived. Yohana, however, was run over by the truck that hit them and his skull was crushed, killing him immediately. A police truck brought them both to the hospital in Karatu.

Laizer was at work when he got the call. He rushed home and contacted Julius and a few other friends in Tanzania to let them know and mobilize a plan. Because the doctors planned on cutting off Supuk's injured leg, Laizer had to hurry. His first action was to wire money to Julius so that Supuk could be transferred to a more advanced hospital in Arusha, where they might be able to save his leg.

Carrying the burden of his family's medical, financial, and social issues from half a world away brought Laizer almost to a breaking point. He had just been able to get his father out of the hospital as his brother was going in. And now he was without his best friend and too far away to do anything for Yohana's family. Laizer needed to find a way to fly home and be with his family.

27

L AIZER LONGED TO VISIT HOME MORE often. He also longed
to find a way for his new friends in the United States to
gain some understanding of his homeland and culture. But
how? The answer came from a brainstorm with Jill Engelstad,
the friend Laizer had met at a dinner party three years earlier,
on the eve of her departure for safari in Tanzania.

Since meeting Laizer, Jill had begun a graduate degree in
global affairs with the goal of improving the quality of life for
people living in extremely impoverished areas. Jill would often
consult with Laizer about her research and ideas. It started
when she was researching the idea of developing mobile drug
stores to transport medicine and other goods to rural areas,
where even basic provisions were lacking.

"What would be the most important things to have in my
mobile wellness market to enhance the health of the people
in your village?" Jill asked. "What about diapers?"

"What they need is medicine," he replied.

And that started a conversation about what his villagers
could do if they were empowered with some basic items. Laizer
and Jill quickly found that they enjoyed discussing problems

and debating solutions with one another. What began as a collaboration quickly evolved into a powerful friendship.

It also mattered that Jill had not only traveled to Laizer's country but had taken great interest in it.

"Dave and I never got to the Serengeti. Will you take us, introduce us to your family, and show us your angan'g?" Jill asked.

The more they discussed the details of the trip, such as what time of year would work best, the more they wondered whether others would also be interested in going. They soon came up with the idea of forming a travel group of twelve people, including himself and Kim, that would pay for Laizer's plane ticket and expenses in exchange for his personal touch on the ground in Tanzania. It was a win on several levels: it got Laizer home, it gave Julius more work, it provided the Americans with a local's perspective on the country, and it provided Laizer an opportunity to create a bridge between his two worlds.

Once they solidified a plan, it took off. Kim was so well connected that once she put the word out, they had twelve people commit to the trip in less than four weeks. They then worked on getting the visas and planning the trip. Jill and Dave hosted a pretrip get-together. The group chemistry was fantastic. It was a great mix of people who got along well. Laizer provided everyone with a list of items to bring and asked them all to carry an extra suitcase of supplies that the people in his village needed, including baby blankets, clothes, and notebooks. The group gathered what was needed and eagerly awaited their departure.

28

I N JANUARY, THE GROUP LANDED IN Arusha. In addition to
Laizer and Kim, there were ten others, including Laizer's
good friend and idea partner, Jill Englestad. Once in Arusha,
Laizer introduced the group to Julius, whose tour company
would lead their trip. Julius had prepared all the details of the
safari. By now he was a seasoned safari guide and well-versed
in the ways of foreigners. The energy among the group was
high and enthusiastic for this long-anticipated adventure.

For Laizer, there was a feeling of optimism that a new
chapter was opening in his life. Here he was in his homeland
of Tanzania with his American wife and friends from the
United States. Beside him was his dear friend Julius, who
had traveled the emotional journey with him from secondary
school to falling for Gracie and then marrying Kim. Julius
had supported Laizer during his departure from—and return
to—his land and people. A sense of "Wow!" coursed through
Laizer's head and heart.

The group spent their first day in Arusha, visiting a large
vegetable market and resting from jetlag. The next morning,
they left early for the Serengeti. Between Kim and Laizer,

everyone was able to be in the loop about their plans. They went through the Serengeti and Ngorongoro, and every day they would head out and have adventures, then come back to a communal supper. The cooks were top notch. Everyone in the group had different interests, and the guides somehow got them all what they wanted. They saw all the cats and the famous wildebeest migration. Some people saw Olduvai Gorge and others went hiking.

The highlight, however, was bringing the group to Laizer's village of Naiyobi. Before that day, few people from outside the village had ever spent time in Naiyobi besides the NCAA rangers, the teachers, and the pastors. There had been tourists, like the German group from Laizer's childhood who passed through on hikes between Empakai Crater and Lake Natron. But the area was too remote for most people. Even that day, Laizer's group almost didn't make it because the road was too muddy to drive the Land Rovers all the way to Naalamala's angan'g. But Laizer did some quick problem-solving and decided the group could camp in "downtown" Naiyobi near the ranger station instead. There, the group would be able to access water and would only have a thirty-minute walk to his mother's angan'g.

Somewhere along the way, Laizer changed from his western clothing into his orkarasha. But what was more subtle, yet not lost on anyone in the group, was that his demeanor also changed. He became more serious, more tuned in to the land, and more ready to lead. They all remarked on how seamlessly he had shifted into his traditional Maasai role right before their eyes.

As soon as the vehicles were parked and everyone emerged, they were surrounded by a horde of children. Some were laughing and playing, and others were hiding behind friends, but all stared inquisitively at the group. As the Americans walked the path to Naalamala's angan'g, they were also joined by at least fifty women adorned in their finest beadwork, their voices lifted in song.

"Kim, they are welcoming you back," Laizer said.

When they arrived at Naalamala's angan'g, she came out and gave Kim a hug, which Laizer said was a big deal because his mother didn't usually hug people.

After a quick round of introductions, the group returned to camp for dinner and then distributed the clothing and blankets they had brought to the dozens of villagers gathered around them. At first, it was pure mayhem, but then Laizer organized everyone, from tiny children to the elderly. One by one, each villager came up to Laizer to receive an item. Blankets were the most coveted items among the mothers, while children were excited to receive items of clothing. Once a child received an article of clothing, he or she put it on and never took it off again during the group's visit.

Part of Laizer's preparations included organizing a market where Maasai women could sell their beaded items to the group. The women sat in a large circle on the ground with their jewelry spread in front of them and Ol Doinyo Lengai towering behind them. It was a scene of color and creativity, and Laizer moved quickly among those in the group to introduce, translate, and encourage connection.

On the second day, Laizer introduced the group to Maasai culture. The group went into a pen where they kept the animals, so one warrior could take a bull and demonstrate how they nick the jugular with an arrow tip, bleed it, and give it to the elders to drink. Then a few women demonstrated beading to the group, during which a local man who had never seen it joined them to watch. The afternoon ended with all the warriors dancing and jumping. At first, the group of Americans just watched, but once Laizer joined in, the rest of the group also joined and they all danced together.

That evening, the group spent time in Naalamala's dark, smoky enkaji with her, one of her sisters, and one of the guides to act as a translator. It wasn't long before the conversation shifted to children, and it was revealed that not one of the twelve Americans in the group had children. The Americans explained to their hosts about birth control, and their hosts were incredulous that anyone would even want to use it. Soon after, the conversation shifted to female circumcision. The Maasai hosts explained how it was done, and Naalamala even showed her guests a rusty razorblade, which she explained would be cleaned off when it was time to circumcise one of her daughters. This time, it was the Americans who responded with incredulity.

Later, Jill described the experience to Laizer as, "The most frank give-and-take on cultural norms between women I could ever imagine. I kept thinking, 'Am I really having this experience?' It was the most fascinating part of the whole trip."

When Laizer asked Naalamala what she thought of the visit, she told him she couldn't believe that none of them had children. But mostly she was grateful to meet the people who had made it possible for him to come home.

29

THIS GROUP OF FRIENDS WAS MUCH more engaged, curious, and compassionate than the groups Laizer had been used to leading, but even they couldn't begin to know what was going on behind the scenes of that idyllic landscape. After they left, Laizer remained in Tanzania to focus on his family again. His first task was to pay his respects to Yohana's wife, Christine, and their two-year-old daughter. He traveled to their village of Loliondo with his brother, Loserian, walking the roughly sixty miles each way. The trip took two days, but once they arrived, they stayed for a week to visit and help out.

Laizer felt so much guilt that Yohana's death had happened while traveling to visit Mekuru. He knew life would be hard for Christine and her daughter. As a Maasai widow, she could not remarry. Instead, she became the property of Yohana's brother, who already had other wives and children to support. Knowing this situation would make it nearly impossible for Christine's daughter to attend school, Laizer offered to sponsor her the way he had been sponsored. It was a kind gesture that allowed Christine to hold onto hope for the future. At the end of the week, they said their goodbyes and Laizer and Loserian walked the two days back to Naiyobi.

Meanwhile, Kim hadn't left with the other Americans. While Laizer and his brother traveled to Loliondo, Kim remained in Naiyobi for those two weeks to get to know the women in her husband's family. Not speaking the language or having grown up with Maasai traditions, Kim wasn't exactly sure what to expect from her visit with her in-laws, but she was determined to put her fear aside and use love as the bedrock of her communication. Knowing this would be a challenging experience, her friends had hid notes of support in Kim's luggage before they left.

Laizer also knew it would be challenging, and before he left for Loliondo with Loserian, he built Kim a primitive latrine, which he would rebuild for her each time she visited from then on. As he shoveled out the latrine, Laizer explained its function to his friends and family in Naiyobi, all of whom found it an oddity.

Kim ended up spending most of her time with one of Laizer's younger sisters, Niomomo. Niomomo was full of life, a gifted athlete, and a talented singer. She was also fourteen and just through puberty, which meant her circumcision and marriage were imminent. Under a new governmental program that offered schooling to all children, Niomomo had been to primary school and would have been eligible for free secondary school had she performed well on standardized testing. But she hadn't.

This was not unusual for Maasai girls, as they often fell behind in their studies because of the many chores they had to complete before and after school. Like Laizer had done for Yohana's daughter, Kim offered to sponsor Niomomo's secondary school. This would also allow Niomomo to avoid circumcision and marriage for another four years or more. Niomomo tentatively agreed.

When Laizer returned, he sat down with Niomomo to discuss the terms of her additional schooling. He was firm: if Kim sponsored Niomomo, Niomomo must agree to study hard and not become pregnant. At this, Niomomo started to waiver. She already had low confidence in her ability to succeed in school and knew that secondary school, taught in English, would be even harder. It would also require her to be far from home. If she were to avoid circumcision, she would even need to stay at school during breaks and holidays. That meant separation from her family, deep homesickness, and the inability to help her mother or grandmother. Niomomo declined the offer.

In spite of their language barrier, Kim persisted in trying to explain the benefits of schooling through pantomime and stilted conversations, but Niomomo continued to refuse. Even when Kim emphasized that Niomomo would have food every day and not have to endure a starvation season, Niomomo declined. When Kim walked away from the angan'g that day, it was with great sadness. For although she understood that loyalty to family was paramount in Niomomo's decision, Kim also understood that without schooling, circumcision and subsequent marriage would be in Niomomo's near future.

Laizer and Kim discussed Niomomo's situation long into the night. How could Niomomo, who had never left Naiyobi, possibly grasp that what she would learn in school could be critical to living a longer, healthier life? How could she know about women's rights, HIV prevention, and nutrition if she hadn't yet been exposed to them? How could she know that school would provide her with a pathway to have choices in the future when she didn't even understand that her culture and climate were changing? And, more poignantly, how could a fourteen-year-old girl compare the benefits school would bring to the cost of leaving a home she knew and loved?

In Naiyobi, no one had ever avoided circumcision. Perhaps to Niomomo, the idea of waiting for circumcision was appealing, but avoiding it altogether was frightening. Perhaps it wasn't appealing at all. After all, circumcision was a rite of passage to adulthood, the pathway to marriage and children, and one of the cornerstones of Maasai society. And getting married later and having fewer children would have stood in contrast to all the cultural values with which Niomomo had been raised. While only a handful of tribes in Tanzania practice female circumcision—including the Maasai, the Sukuma, and the Sonjo—without exposure to any of the numerous other tribes, Maasai girls in remote villages like Naiyobi do not even know that not being circumcised is an option.

Within two weeks of Laizer and Kim's return to the United States, Laizer received his Friday night call. It was from his mother, who already missed him and wondered when he would be back. Laizer loved to hear her voice but was also comfortable in the home he and Kim had made for themselves in Foresta, with its soft beds and fully stocked refrigerator. They chatted a bit about the visit, but then Naalamala paused. She clearly had news to share. When she started speaking again, she confessed that Niomomo was getting ready for her marriage and then quickly ended the call. Laizer locked eyes with Kim, who knew what had happened without Lazier uttering a word. Together they cried, as both of their hearts were broken.

30

Laizer and Kim were getting comfortable in their California lives. Both worked steady jobs, and although they hadn't yet bought a house, they at least had a long-term rental, a difficult prize to find where they lived. Soon, perhaps, they might consider adopting kids. But they were in no hurry as they were enjoying life.

Laizer also was enjoying all the technology available to him in the United States, especially the convenience of his car. One Saturday, Laizer woke early to drive the two hours to Manteca to upgrade his cell phone. Kim stayed behind because she was recovering from hip surgery—the type of surgery that one simply couldn't get in Tanzania because the country lacked the necessary resources. It was summer, which meant hot and dry weather, but neither of them thought much of it as Laizer drove away.

While he was heading back into the mountains toward home with a new cell phone, he noticed smoke plumes in the direction of Foresta. He sped up, but it was another half hour before he would arrive. When he did, he ran into the house and alerted Kim about the smoke. She had just heard that there was a fire in the area but that it was still far away. Concerned but not yet too worried, Laizer and Kim began having lunch. Then there was a knock at the door. A voice shouted that the fire was fast approaching. Laizer ran outside, and his eyes immediately began stinging from the smoke. The fire was rapidly advancing from the canyon below, racing up the dry mountainside, burning everything in its path.

With only enough time to grab a few bags of clothes, sleeping bags, and a computer, Laizer and Kim rushed out to their cars. Kim was limping from surgery, but she could drive. Laizer yelled for Kim to go, but Kim refused to leave until she knew Laizer was safely in his car. It was fortunate she waited because Laizer couldn't find his keys, and she had an extra set. As they raced their cars away from the house, the fire closed in and enveloped their home. They parked a safe distance away as fire consumed it. Laizer tried to return to protect the house, but the fire personnel wouldn't let him through. There was nothing he could have done against this powerful force. Instead, all Laizer could do was join Kim and stare in horror as their house and nearly everything dear to them burned to the ground.

Almost everything was destroyed, including irreplaceable items such as photos, journals, school certificates, and the lovely beaded wedding dress. The only material possessions they had left were their cars, the few things they had grabbed, and Laizer's new cell phone. Now they had no house and no possessions. That night they slept in Kim's office—or, at least, attempted to sleep; Kim cried all night. Finding another house in their town would be nearly impossible, and they didn't have the savings to replace the material items they had lost. Homeless yet loved, Laizer and Kim stayed with Jill and Dave for almost six weeks while two other friends, Joy and Katie, started a Go Fund Me drive that eventually raised twenty thousand dollars for the couple. It was a stunning gesture of support from a community that had embraced them.

Unfortunately, money didn't make finding housing any easier. One other couple who had also lost their home in the fire was given temporary park housing because they worked for the National Park Service, but Laizer and Kim did not have that privilege. There simply was nothing available for Laizer and Kim to rent in the area, and buying was too expensive. They began a period of bouncing from place to place, trying to find a home. If they couldn't find a house in their little community, where would they live?

31

OVER THE NEXT FIVE YEARS, AS Laizer and Kim's personal goals became increasingly clear, the steps to achieving these goals became increasingly unclear. Before they could take on children, they wanted to own a home. Before they could own a home, they needed to find a community that had wide open spaces and welcomed their interracial marriage. In addition to personal goals, they also held an overarching desire to aid the Maasai community, not just for altruistic purposes, but also because Laizer, as Mekuru's oldest son, had an obligation to help. But before Laizer and Kim could achieve anything, they needed employment that would pay enough to buy a home and provide enough flexibility for visits to Naiyobi. Their current jobs provided some flexibility but didn't pay nearly enough to help them afford a home. How would it all be possible?

They started with little steps. With each trip back to Naiyobi, Laizer would fix up his family members' homes a bit more. First, he brought in a bed and couch for his mother. Next, he installed a solar panel on her enkaji so she could charge her cellular phone and a small television set Laizer had bought her that she used to watch DVDs of Maasai dance videos. Then he poured a cement floor for her, which Naalamala thought was cold but which Laizer liked because it cut down on the dust. As much as Laizer loved tinkering with his mother's enkaji to make it more comfortable, he was eager to take on bigger projects to help the rest of his family and his community.

Yet the more Laizer and Kim thought about how to help, the more they were overwhelmed with the vast array of issues the Maasai faced, most of which stemmed from the core issue of land use limitations. Not only had the Maasai been relocated from their historic lands, but they were increasingly boxed in by parks, cities, the burgeoning flower industry, and game reserves. The Maasai people's traditional process of rotating cattle through the plains, which once ensured that grazing wouldn't damage the land, were now restricted. As a result, overgrazing was common, as was food scarcity.

Overgrazing, food scarcity, disease—all of these issues have increased rapidly due to two compounding threats: population growth and climate change. Exponential population growth, driven by a cultural tradition of early marriage, lack of birth control, and a tradition of valuing children as wealth, has led to more pressure on already-limited food resources. Climate change, driven by forces outside the control of the Maasai, has led to even further reduced availability of these resources.

As a result of these compounding stressors, many Maasai are now leaving their villages to find work in cities. With no education or transferable skills, Maasai men often end up working as guards, which are tedious, poorly paid jobs. Maasai women who move to the city often end up working as prostitutes. In addition to the emotional and familial burdens prostitution causes, it is one of the ways in which HIV is transferred from cities to rural areas—made worse by the Maasai's polygamous society. When Maasai are undernourished, they are more vulnerable to HIV, as well as to many other diseases, including tuberculosis, cholera, malaria, and worms. Further, many elderly people lose their eyesight late in life to glaucoma, trachoma, or cataracts, making them dependent upon the younger generation.

Before developing a strategy to aid the Maasai, Laizer and Kim considered those already made by the government and large nonprofit groups to determine what had and hadn't been effective. While it is the government that has dramatically limited the Maasai people's access to grazing lands, it is also the government that has the greatest ability to help the Maasai improve their lives and opportunities. Yet, as is true in so many places, the government has proven to be an unreliable protector in Naiyobi.

The government jumped in to finish building a clinic the villagers had started, but haven't followed through by reliably staffing it with a doctor or supplying it with medicine. The government created a road, but after every heavy rain, it is an unusable mess. The government provides deliveries of grain, but only when the road is passable. There is a school and free education, but attendance requires a uniform that most Maasai cannot afford.

The government has introduced some targeted solutions to Maasai communities, including Naiyobi, but they have often failed to achieve their goals and have even made things worse. To target sexually transmitted diseases, the government provided sexual education in a language that the community doesn't speak. To target pestilence, the government has allowed the sale of poisons without any instruction about dilution or toxicity. The government made female circumcision illegal but ignores the fact that the Maasai now circumcise girls at even younger ages to avoid detection.

Worst of all—according to Laizer—is the threat that the government, through the NCAA, will force more Maasai communities to move out of the NCA. If that happens, those forced out might end up in cities where their skills are not transferable or in rural areas that have limited water, dangerous diseases such as malaria, extreme temperatures, and little forage for their cattle. If those same Maasai had education, training, or money, they would have more control over their lives if such a situation came to pass. Many might even proactively choose to leave the NCA. Without education, training, or money, however, they remain vulnerable to the whims of the government.

Despite their intentions to help, nonprofit organizations can be another unreliable protector of the Maasai in Tanzania. Why? More often than not, representatives show up and make promises but never return to implement any solutions. In cases where there is follow-through, an initial effort is usually made to set up systems for such activities as collecting rain or efficiently cooking meals, but less often are there any mechanisms to repair those systems when they break down. This leaves the women with no option other than to go back to walking many miles to collect water and wood. As a result, well-intentioned efforts to help the Maasai and other tribes often fail.

However, Laizer and Kim noted that one model of providing assistance had been more successful than others: the long-term adoption of a village by an outside organization.

While this assistance model hasn't been applied much in Tanzania—particularly in places as remote as Naiyobi—it has been successfully employed several times in Kenya. Given that Laizer and Kim wanted to focus their efforts in Naiyobi, they were invigorated with hopes of success.

To move forward, Laizer and Kim didn't allow themselves to become overwhelmed with the myriad issues the Maasai faced and instead picked one area of focus. Although they discussed the options at great length, there was never really any question as to where they would start, which would be with a focus on women's rights and girls' education. Empowering women and giving them choices would benefit the entire community, and educating girls is known to be the surest way to slow population growth. Empowering women would also provide those women with the tools they needed to live outside Naiyobi, if they chose to do so or were forced to do so by the government.

Of course, as part of this, Laizer and Kim knew they would be taking a stand on some of the Maasai's most sacred traditions, such as female circumcision, arranged marriage, and the emphasis on having many children. As such, they thought a lot about how these and other changes might affect Maasai culture. Would the Maasai emphasis on family, community, and impromptu hospitality remain? Would the Maasai's light footprint on the earth, with each person leaving almost no waste on the land, continue? Would the Maasai still look to the open, starry sky for wisdom?

They also thought a lot about potential short-term consequences of shifting gender roles. If warriors were replaced by police, and elders were replaced by elected councils, would men feel they had a meaningful role in the Maasai community? Would men be able to develop strong bonds across their age sets without serving as warriors? Would they even have age sets? If women were educated and moved to the city for work, who would take on the role of caring for the children and keeping the family together? Would women miss their communities of extended family surrounded by open skies and clean air? And, perhaps most centrally, at what point might changes to traditional practices leave the Maasai no longer feeling grounded in their culture?

32

THE TRUTH THAT LAIZER AND KIM have come to accept is that Maasai culture is changing anyway. If one visits Maasai villages in Kenya, the change is further along. Clothes are now made in China; homes are now made of brick with metal roofs; people speak in both Swahili and Maa; and religion may be the traditional belief in Engai, Christian, or Islamic. Even in remote Naiyobi, where the government has mandated that nothing is to change, changes are happening. There is now cellular service closer to town. The ranger station gets CNN with a satellite dish. Lions are protected by the government.

Meanwhile, the NCAA is starting to expand the boundaries of the NCA, once again restricting agriculture and discussing moving more residents out of the conservation area. Water is also becoming less available due to outside forces, including use by the high-end safari lodges and, of course, climate change. Because of these changes, Laizer and Kim were drawn to empowering the Maasai people of Naiyobi to take charge of their own paths and prevent themselves from being vulnerable to the changes coming. It was time to get started.

Laizer and Kim started hosting American groups traveling to Tanzania each year. During each trip, they would experiment with ways to intervene in aspects of Maasai life. They started by supporting education. While the government was now providing free primary school to all Tanzanian citizens, attendance still required uniforms, which cost money. Laizer, having been sponsored himself, began paying it forward. Laizer had already paid for Yohana's child and then for his own brother, Parsanga, to go to secondary school. Now he started paying for other girls to attend.

When Jill Engelstad came on Laizer's first trip and learned about their mission, she also began sponsoring girls. Soon others did as well. Trip participants also brought items to support the students, such as mattresses, and to support the teachers, with supplies such as a microscope one participant brought for a classroom.

Once Laizer and Kim got started, additional means of assistance revealed themselves. Kim began working with Julius's wife, a bright and talkative Maasai woman named Theresia. Theresia lived in Arusha but had grown up in a Maasai village and spoke Swahili, Maa, and English.

Together, Kim and Theresia interviewed the Maasai women about what they wanted in life. They asked them about their greatest needs and challenges, how they felt about education, whether they wanted courses focusing on a range of women's issues, and whether they wanted to learn Swahili. Prior to these interviews, no one had ever asked any of the Maasai in Naiyobi, let alone the women, what they wanted. It turned out the women were very motivated to learn all the topics suggested and gain financial independence. Bolstered with this knowledge, Kim and Theresia started to offer the women courses, and the women came en masse.

Meanwhile, Laizer knew the Maasai needed representation in government, especially with the decisions that would have an impact on the community in the future. Starting to collaborate with leadership in the NCAA, Laizer suggested entering a sister-park arrangement with Yosemite. The idea was to shine a spotlight on the Maasai, to ensure they received fair treatment while helping the NCAA gain access to training, resources, and experts who would enact further conservation measures for the Maasai's well-being. To ensure he would be seen as a legitimate voice among the Naiyobi villagers, Laizer kept twenty-five cattle in Naiyobi, always dressed in his orkarasha while there, and listened to the concerns of the men by meeting with his family and other men in the community. He leaned on Theresia and Kim to meet with the women and then discuss their needs with him.

Over and over again, Laizer heard from the men that the community needed more food and that the people were unprepared to move out of the NCA. What Laizer did not hear was a clamoring to expand women's education or provide for women's rights. He certainly didn't hear it from Mekuru, who seemed to dig even more deeply into his traditions as the world changed around him. But Theresia did. And Kim did. And, finally, Laizer did too.

When he listened carefully, his younger sisters started whispering to him hesitantly, asking for help in making change even as their father took on his seventh wife. And women from the village started seeking him out when he was home, asking whether he could sponsor their daughters to go to school. Even Naalamala, who was at first incredulous that the American visitors would purposely avoid circumcision or use birth control, started opening up to the idea of more rights for women.

And it was none too soon. Once again, drought had led to widespread hunger. Although the NCAA was supposed to deliver food to Naiyobi to offset the restriction against cultivation, the dirt road was continually washing out, and deliveries rarely occurred. Worse, the NCAA was once again enforcing restrictions on grazing and cultivation. And the clinic still had no doctor and no medicine. Urgency to help the people of Naiyobi brought Laizer and Kim even more clarity and motivation to act.

33

Meanwhile, Laizer's time as a warrior was coming to an end. Had he lived in Tanzania, this transition would have been marked by the last of the major coming-of-age ceremonies, the *eunoto*, when a warrior becomes an *imorruk*, or elder. It is the time for an age set to renew their bonds and move into leadership roles. It is an emotional transition, as being a warrior is a grueling but an exciting time of life. Once a young man becomes a junior elder, it is time to get married and have a family. He now owns cattle and becomes part of the decision-making body of the community because, traditionally, there is no other government or law enforcement. It is less glamorous than being a warrior but serves an equally important function in Maasai culture.

As with other major life events that affect an age set, the chief of the warrior age set sits with the elders and tells them the warriors are ready. The elders approach the Laiboni, who decides whether it is time by tossing pebbles and reading the patterns they make. Over beers, the Laiboni meets with the elders to tell them when eunoto will occur, and runners spread the news. The warriors arrive in single file throughout the day. By the time the ceremony starts the following morning, over a thousand warriors will have arrived from hundreds of miles in every direction.

Had Laizer been in Naiyobi, Naalamala would have sat him down, lathered him up, and shaved his head one last time—removing the braids and yarn that he would have worn proudly as a warrior. She then would have rubbed ochre all over his head. Laizer would have donned a feathered headdress, painted his face white, and stood in a line with the other warriors, framed by the backdrop of Ol Doinyo Lengai and surrounded by women in their stunning hand-beaded white. But he wasn't there; he was with his wife in the United States.

So the ceremony went on without him. Although tradition said that none of the warriors should have married until they were elders, several men in Laizer's group were already married. During the ceremony, these wives—which would have included Kim—walked up to their husbands, took off their belts, and let the belts fall to the ground—unless a wife had cheated. If so, she could not touch the belt; if she did, she would be cursed and might soon die. In fact, to even attend the ceremony, the wives who cheated had to pay fines in cattle (as would the men with whom they'd cheated). Once they paid, these women were able to join the ceremony.

At the end of the ceremony, the warriors laid down their spears and took up wooden staffs to symbolize their transition from warriorhood to elder and cattle owner. The ceremony then morphed into a multiday event. The new elders slaughtered cattle and feasted on the meat. The elders blessed the new junior elders by spitting on them. Then there were dancing, jumping, and festivities that lasted for several days.

After the ceremony, the junior elders no longer lived warrior lives. They were each given an inaugural herd of cattle by their families and were finally allowed to eat meat in the presence of women. Ritual marriage for Laizer's age set was then opened for the warriors who were not already married, with their fathers arranging the matches. Had Laizer followed the path of his father's choosing, he would have been getting ready to marry Mekuru's friend's daughter, who was only fourteen.

But Laizer wasn't there, and he wasn't following the path his father had laid out. He was in Yosemite, married to Kim and following his own path. Yet Laizer was careful to honor his mother by paying her a fine of one cow for not being there. Custom dictated that Laizer, as the firstborn, must be the first one of Naalamala's sons to transition to junior elder, so this payment allowed his mother to present her other sons without him there. The next time he was home, Laizer would let his mother shave him ceremonially. In a merging of modern and traditional cultures, one of Laizer's age mates recorded the event on his cell phone and texted it to Laizer.

Even though Laizer did not attend the ceremony, the timing for the rite of passage resonated. Laizer and Kim had finally found their own place to live, albeit a rental, and were considering adoption. Laizer was enjoying his employment and had even won an employee-of-the-year award for his organization. While he was still underemployed, both in terms of challenge and salary, he at least felt valued. It was also about this time that Laizer became involved in setting up a sister-park arrangement between Yosemite and the NCA—a huge vote of confidence from the two land-management organizations that were central to his life.

Meanwhile, Kim had made it through a ceremony of her own—the completion of a graduate program focusing on international, community-based conservation. After spending more time with the women of Naiyobi, Kim was motivated to attend graduate school and learn how she could best help them. She enrolled in a Master of Arts program in biological sciences education through Miami University of Ohio, which offered an international field-based degree.

Through the program, Kim was able to focus her assignments and projects on women-centered education, training, and development. Although she studied groups around the world, Kim spent the majority of her time researching ways to assist the women of Naiyobi. One of these was microloans, which have had various levels of success in other impoverished cultures. What if they were given to the women of Naiyobi? It was time to find out.

34

LAIZER AND KIM DEVISED A THREE-PART plan to direct their assistance toward Naiyobi. To begin implementing their plan, they set up a community-based organization called "Nadupoi," meaning "live forever," "resistant," or "not easily broken." Through Nadupoi, they could fulfill their first two objectives: sending kids to school and supporting women's empowerment through training and economic development. The third part of their plan involved providing the Maasai a representative voice in government. Laizer planned to run for political office to be that voice.

They were off to a good start toward their first goal. Several kids had already been sponsored to attend school, with two women even in college. During this time, the government also began offering free secondary school—so sponsors only needed to pay for room and board, uniforms, bedding, school supplies, and transportation. That total cost was equivalent to about $400 USD—way too much for most Maasai, but one which many sponsors were happy to fund. In addition to providing financial support, Laizer became a steady source of emotional support for these children, checking in with them each year to see how they were faring emotionally.

To prevent girls from being rushed into circumcision when they were home from school, Laizer tried to find safe places for the girls to stay during school breaks. He couldn't find places for all the girls, but at least some were able to stay away and avoid being forced into circumcision and marriage. And, for the first time, there was the possibility that Maasai girls from Naiyobi would mature into women without circumcision. The precedent for more girls to follow in their footsteps had been set.

They were also off to a strong start toward their second goal. With Kim and Theresia's assistance, the women of Naiyobi started a savings-and-loan program by creating a community bank. A rotating fund with seed money from Laizer and Kim's friends was used to support the development of women's small business cooperatives. Start-ups included co-ops to sell corn, beans, salt, rice, and even sheep and goats. Concurrently, Kim and Theresia offered a range of classes to empower the women. To maximize the success of the women's businesses, they taught classes in math, money management, and small business practices. There were also classes on malaria, invasive plant identification, and reproductive health. Theresia later learned that the women were successful in implementing strategies learned through these classes, which not only made her and Kim feel good about the changes they were enacting, but also motivated them to offer more.

For the third part of the plan, Laizer was going to run for counselor of the Naiyobi ward. The position would involve representing three villages for a five-year term. Kim even agreed to live in Tanzania for this period if Laizer were elected. Everything was in place, but even the most careful planning couldn't have accounted for the COVID-19 pandemic of 2020. After delaying the trip by two months, Lazier decided he had to try to execute his plan. He quit his job, boarded a plan, changed into his orkarasha, and transitioned toward life in his other world. Kim stayed in the United States.

On the ground, Laizer had to hurry—not only did he have to get to Loliondo to register to run for office, but he also needed to campaign in all three villages. Yet he couldn't hurry. There was no bus service between villages, and Laizer had no car. So, as he had throughout his life, he walked.

He walked across the open plains and felt the freshness of the air in the Great Rift Valley. For safety, he planned on walking only in the day, but he often started when the moon was still high in the open sky. Once again, he was amid the familiar antelope and occasional elephants of this landscape—but, thankfully, no lions or leopards. One day, he traveled with two other men who were headed in the same direction. He was so hot, he took off his underwear, and they laughed, asking, "What are you wearing?"

Everywhere he went, he talked to villagers. Laizer discussed his plans to represent them—to give them a voice, a chance. And he listened. He listened to their dreams and their fears and what they needed to be successful in a changing world. But Laizer should have started months earlier. Walking was slow and the distances were vast. He finally procured a Land Rover to get around, but it was too late; many of the people whose votes he needed had already promised their votes to other candidates.

Partway through the campaign, Kim was furloughed from her job due to the pandemic restrictions. She found a friend to sublet their rental and joined Laizer in Tanzania. A few years earlier, Laizer had bought land in Mto wa Mbu and built a home as a surprise for Kim. Mto wa Mbu is close enough to Naiyobi to visit frequently, large enough to offer potential employment for both Laizer and Kim, and safe enough to allow Kim more freedom.

The home was a useful base for the months they spent there together and would have been invaluable had Laizer won. However, as COVID-19 would do to so many plans that year, Laizer's plan to get elected was derailed. He simply couldn't make up for lost time. Another candidate won by just three votes. Laizer and Kim stayed in Tanzania for a few more months, helping their family and community before heading back to Yosemite.

The return was bittersweet. The land, as always, was welcoming, as was the community. And they had a place to live, since Kim hadn't given up their rental. But Laizer had given up the job he liked to run for political office, and the job he found upon returning to the U.S. was not fulfilling, paid poorly, and required sitting in traffic to get home—an irony of living and working in a national park. Although Kim was happily back in her former job, she knew it would soon be time to move on. With open hearts, Kim and Laizer decided to embrace their Yosemite home, knowing it would soon be time to take another chance and write the next chapters of their lives together.

Epilogue

HUMBLE AND RESILIENT LIKE HIS MOTHER while shouldering great responsibilities like his father, Laizer will continue to bring improvements to his birthplace. He remains optimistic, even though the goals of achieving equality for the Maasai women and converting his community into a thriving, self-sufficient village sometimes seem unachievable. With his innate ability to unite people from radically different ethnic and economic backgrounds, this next chapter of Laizer's life promises to be full of transformation, hope, and prosperity.

Nadupoi

NADUPOI IS A GOVERNMENT-RECOGNIZED, COMMUNITY-BASED ORGANIZATION. Its mission is to provide the women of Naiyobi with opportunities for education, training, and economic development to foster their well-being.

www.Nadupoi.weebly.com

Gratitude

Chuck Carter, Stephanie Dolreny, Jill Engelstad, Emma Loss, Joy Marshall, Allan Mazur, Linda Mazzu, Aloyce Mtui, Paul Ollig, Leslie Paladino, Lisa Rhudy, Michael Ross, Winston Seiler, Michelle Sims, Andy Steele, Molly Stephens, John Sturdevant, Max Sturdevant, Wren Sturdevant, Julie Mazur Tribe, Margy Verba, Erik Westerlund, and Catherine Williams all either shared stories about Laizer, provided comments on the text and suggestions on the format, or encouraged me in the completion of this project. I am grateful for their support.

Sarah Katreen Hoggatt and Jessica Santina at Lucky Bat Books shared their expertise to make the book complete.

Wendy Mckellar, Dayna Higgins, Kim Laizer, and Winston Seiler made the book beautiful through artwork, map-making, and photography.

Kelly Phillipson edited several drafts of the book. She not only provided writing assistance, but she also inspired me to think more deeply about the themes touched upon in the book. The final product is so much better due to her excellent help.

Dr. Terrance McCabe and Dr. Richard Waller generously reviewed portions of the book for historical and cultural accuracy. I appreciate their corrections and learning from the depth and breadth of knowledge they have from decades of research on East African pastoralists.

John, Max, and Wren Sturdevant sat with me while Laizer told his stories and encouraged me to finish writing the book. The only reason this book is complete is because of their interest and insistence I complete what I started. I adore these three more than they know.

Kim Laizer allowed me to enter her personal world. She is openhearted, brave, and incredibly generous. Her trust in me to tell the story of her and Laizer is humbling.

My greatest thanks go to Olotumi Laizer. He shared the stories of his life with me as well as his hopes and dreams. Not only is Laizer a fascinating person, but he is also a wonderful friend. I hope I have done his story justice.

References

African Population and Health Research Center (APHRC). *Population and Health Dynamics in Nairobi's Informal Settlements: Report of the Nairobi Cross-sectional Slums Survey (NCSS) 2012*. Nairobi, Kenya: APHRC, 2014.

Amin, M., Willets, D. and J. Eames. *The Last of the Maasai*. Nairobi, Kenya: Camerapix Publishers International, 1987.

Buzinde, C. N., Kalavar, J. M., and K. Melubo. 2014. "Tourism and community well-being: The case of the Maasai in Tanzania." *Annals of Tourism Research* 44 (2014): 20-35.

Charney, S. "From nature tourism to ecotourism? The case of the Ngorongoro Conservation Area, Tanzania." *Human Organization* 64 (2005): 75-88.

Dheer, A., Davidian, E., Jacobs, M. H., Ndorosa, J., Straka, T. M., and O. P. Höner. "Emotions and cultural importance predict the acceptance of large carnivore management strategies by Maasai pastoralists." *Frontiers in Conservation Science* 2 (2021).

Galvin, K., Boone R., and T. J. McCabe. "Transitions in the Ngorongoro Conservation Area: The story of Cultivation and Conservation." In *Serengeti IV*, 483-512. Chicago, Illinois: University of Chicago Press, 2015.

Galvin, K., Thornton, P. K., Boone, R., and J. Sunderland. "Climate variability and impacts on East African livestock herders: The Maasai of Ngorongoro Conservation Area, Tanzania." *African Journal of Range and Forage Science* 21 (2004): 183-189.

Hodgson, D. *Being Maasai, Becoming Indigenous: Postcolonial Politics in a Neoliberal World*. Bloomington, Indiana: Indiana University Press, 2011.

Hodgson, D. *Once Intrepid Warriors: Gender, Ethnicity, and the Cultural Politics of Maasai Development*. Bloomington, Indiana: Indiana University Press, 2001.

Lee, P., Koromo, S., Merdacor, J., and C. Mather. "Scientific facts and oral traditions in Oldumpai Gorge, Tanzania: Symmetrically analyzing palaeoanthropological and Maasai black boxes." *Social Science Information* 58 (2019): 57-83.

Lekuton, J. L. *Facing the Lion*. Washington, D.C.: National Geographic Society, 2003.

Linke, A., Witmer, F., O'Loughlin, J., McCabe, J. Y., and J. Tir. "Drought, Local Institutional Context, and Support for Violence in Kenya." *Journal of Conflict Resolution* 13 (2017).

May, A., and J. T. McCabe. "City Work in a Time of AIDS: Maasai Labor Migration in Tanzania." *Africa Today* 51 (2004): 3-32.

McCabe, J. T. *Cattle Bring Us to Our Enemies: Turkana Ecology, History, and Raiding in a Disequilibrium System*. Ann Arbor, Michigan: University of Michigan Press, 2004.

McCabe, J. T., Leslie, P. and DeLuca, L. "Adopting Cultivation to Remain Pastoralists: the diversification of pastoral livelihoods in northern Tanzania." *Human Ecology* 38 (2010): 321-334.

McCabe, T. J., Smith, N. J., Leslie, P. W., and A. L. Telligman. "Livelihood diversification through migration among a pastoral people: contrasting case studies of Maasai in northern Tanzania." *Human Organization* 73 (2014): 389-400.

Melubo, K., and A. Carr. "Developing indigenous tourism in the *bomas*: critiquing issues from within the Maasai community in Tanzania." *Journal of Heritage Tourism* 14 (2019): 219-232.

Melubo, K., and B. Lovelock. "Living inside a UNESCO world heritage site: the perspective of the Maasai community of Tanzania." *Tourism Planning and Development* 16 (2019): 1-20.

Miller B., Leslie, P., and J. T. McCabe. "Coping with Natural Hazards in a Conservation Context: Resource-Use Decisions of Maasai Households in Recent and Historical Droughts." *Human Ecology* 42 (2014): 753-768.

Misiak, M., Butovskaya, M., and P. Sorokowski. "Ecology shapes moral judgements towards food-wasting behavior: evidence from the Yali of West Papua, the Ngorongoro Maasai, and Poles." *Appetite* 125 (2018): 124-130.

Nelson, F. "Natural conservationists? Evaluating the impact of pastoralist land use practices on Tanzania's wildlife economy." *Pastoralism: Research, Policy, and Practice* 2 (2012): 15.

Ofcansky, T. P. "The 1889-97 rinderpest epidemic and the rise of British and German colonialism in eastern and southern Africa." *Journal of African Studies* 8 (1981): 31-8.

Wa Thiong'o, N. *The River Between*. London, England: Heinemann, 1965.

Ntaiya, K. E. "Warrior's Spirit: the Stories of Four Women from Kenya's Enduring Tribe." Master's thesis, University of Pittsburgh, 2011.

Pangerl, D. *A Full Circle: Walking Alongside Maasai Woman in Tanzania*. Edina, Minnesota: Beaver's Pond Press, Inc., 2012.

Saitoti, Tepilit Ole. *Maasai*. New York: Abradale Press, 1980.

Saitoti, Tepilit Ole. *The Worlds of a Maasai Warrior: An Autobiography*. Berkeley and Los Angeles, California: University of California Press, 1986.

Selemani, I. S. "Indigenous knowledge and rangelands' biodiversity conservation in Tanzania: success and failure." *Biodiversity and Conservation* 29 (2020): 3863-3876.

Spear, T., and R. Waller. (editors) *Being Maasai: Ethnicity and Identity in East Africa*. Athens, Ohio: Ohio University Press, 1993.

Woodhouse, E. and J. T. McCabe. "Well-being and conservation: diversity and change in visions of a good life among the Maasai of northern Tanzania." *Ecology and Society* 23 (2018).

About the Author

Photo: Rachel Mazur and Olotumi Laizer in Naiyobi, Tanzania, in 2016. Credit: Kim Laizer

RACHEL MAZUR IS THE AUTHOR OF *Speaking of Bears: The Bear Crisis and a Tale of Rewilding from Yosemite, Sequoia, and Other National Parks*; *The Nature Club* series for middle-graders; *If You Were a Bear*, and numerous popular and scientific articles. Her day job is as an ecologist for the National Park Service. Rachel lives in Port Angeles, Washington, where she goes adventuring with her husband, John; their kids, Max and Wren; and their dog, Cinnamon.